BILL of RIGHTS for the HARD of HEARING

A demonstration of love toward the hard of hearing in every department of the church

David M. Harrison

Copyright © 2018 David M. Harrison
All rights reserved. This book or any portion thereof may not be reproduced or used in any manner whatsoever without the express written permission of the publisher except for the use of brief quotation in a book review.

Church model created by David M. Harrison
Cover Design and Photography by Pat Morris
Proofreading by Cathy Hart Harrison
Editing by Doreen E. Steele

All scripture quotations are taken from the King James Version and The New International Version

ISBN 9781941749555
Library of Congress Control Number: 2016911748

4-P Publishing
Chattanooga, Tennessee

I am a crusader campaigning for hearing accessibility. I move with an evangelistic fervor proclaiming the need to help those with hearing loss.

Contents

CONTENTS 3

My Tribute: A gift from God 7
A Guest Editor's Thoughts 8

SECTION I "BILL OF RIGHTS FOR THE HARD OF HEARING" . 11

Hello, Can You Hear Me O.K? 12
Purchase an FM system 16
First Impressions of Your Church 16
The Hearing Center 18
    Hearing Center Manager 19
    Registration forms 20
Role of the Pastor 21
The Role of Ushers 22
Classroom Accessibility 23
Prayer time in the church 25
Make Special Events Hearing Accessible 27
Make the Music Hearing Accessible 28
Conduct an All-Church Accessible Workshop 30
Advertise Your Accessible Ministry 31

SECTION II 21 WAYS TO COMMUNICATE WITH HARD OF HEARING 34

Prayer: The most powerful form of communication 35
The CapTel Captioned Telephone 40
    24/7 Help Line 40
    Spanish or English 41
    Clear captioning 45
    Braille Captioned Telephone Hard of Hearing and Blind to Hearing 45
Cell Phone Captioning 47

SORENSON VIDEOPHONE (DEAF TO DEAF IN ASL ONLY)	50
AVA DEAF PERSON TO A HEARING GROUP	53
UBI DUO 2	58
TTY RELAY PHONE CALLS	62
FINGER SPELLING (MANUAL ALPHABET)	64
TOTAL COMMUNICATION	69
SIMULTANEOUS COMMUNICATION,	69
EXPRESSIVE VS. RECEPTIVE COMMUNICATION	70
MANUALLY CODED ENGLISH	70
LIPREADING	71
CUED SPEECH OF LONDON	76
CAPTIONING IN PUBLIC PLACES	78
CAPTIONING IN CHURCHES:	78
CAPTIONING IN THE CLASSROOM	79
TYPE WELL CAPTIONING	79
AUTOMATIC SPEECH RECOGNITION	80
CLASSROOM CAPTIONING	81
CAPTIONING IN WORSHIP SERVICE	82
TEXTING	82
SKYPE	88
SkypeIn	*89*
SkypeOut	*90*
NOTE TAKING	91
"LIP SPEAKING"	92
E-MAIL	94
HOSPITAL COMMUNICATION BOARD	96
SECTION III	**101**
MY SEED DREAM	102
BEFORE I DIE CAMPAIGN	103
AMERICAN DISABILITIES ACT	104
WHAT IS HEARING ACCESSIBILITY?	110
A HEARING ACCESSIBLE CHURCH	114

COMMUNICATION GAP SYNDROME	116
DEFENSIVE HEARING FOR COMMUNICATION	118
FIVE GATES TO BETTER HEARING	121
STUPIDITY PILL	123
GREAT HOPE FOR HEARING LOSS	126
THE GOLDEN RULE	136
MISSION FIELDS IN AMERICA	143
MINISTERING TO SHUTOUTS	149
A PEER SUPPORT MINISTRY	154
STORIES THAT HEAL	158
THE MAGIC BUTTON	166
MY PKT AMPLIFIER STORY	178
THE DREAM TO HEAR	186
ACRES OF DIAMONDS	191
MY DYING WISH FOR YOU	195
MORE INFORMATION ON CAPTIONING	199
Closed Captioning	*199*
Speed Typing	*199*
Open Captioning Movies	*200*
Real-Time Captioning	*200*
Subtitles	*200*
Stage Texting	*201*
Subtitled Cinema	*202*
Get the Script	*203*
C-Print Captioning	*203*
ACKNOWLEDGMENT	**207**
AUTHOR'S PROFILE	**212**

My Tribute: A gift from God

*My deepest gratitude and praise
goes to my Heavenly Father
who redeemed me by the
blood of His Son Jesus Christ.
His love and mercy has never ceased
His Holy Spirit delivered me from the
depression caused by a hearing disability
to a ministry of serving hard of hearing.
Let My People Hear was born after
fourteen days of fasting and prayer:
A mission of helping others find
alternative ways to communicate.
Thanks to the Mighty Holy One
who has done great things through me.
Every day in the Lord is a day
of blessings and miracles untold.
To God be the glory forever and ever.*

*"Whoso offers praise glorifies Me, and to him that
orders his conversation
aright will I show the salvation of God."
Psalm50:23*

A Guest Editor's Thoughts

I understand where David is coming from. The *U.S. Declaration of Independence and Constitution* refer *to* "inalienable" (God-Given, inseparable) rights endowed upon humankind by Our Creator. This includes all people; yet some have been late in gaining rights to "life, liberty, and the pursuit of happiness."

The Americans with Disabilities Act does not apply to churches; still, voluntarily, many churches have built ramps to help their parishioners with mobility disabilities get into the sanctuary. However, once they are in, the job of aiding people with various needs is far from done. Sometimes, churches put written materials in large print versions, so people with declining vision (often, their elderly parishioners) can see.

We are far behind in helping the hard of hearing understand in church. We are good at music: many churches flash lyrics on a big screen. But not sermons? Think about it: *if you can hear and see, which do you rely on more in church, your vision or your hearing?* Close your eyes, and you can hear the message. Pastors ask: Bow your heads and close your eyes in prayer."

Many of us with hearing loss rely on visual cues and lip reading to help "see" what we cannot hear well, or piece together parts we do hear into a somewhat-understandable message. Add in losses of social life at church: yes, even the church family can be impatient with hard of hearing. I experienced this at a young age, but older adults, losing other capacities at the same time, find this far more difficult.

Our charge is of God, who gave us an inalienable "right to become His children." So, He also gave us the means: "by grace, through faith, it is the gift of God (Ephesians 2:8-9) How do we get our faith? Faith come by hearing and hearing by the Word of God" (Romans 10:17) I exhort you, readers: pastors, leaders, lay people, do not leave us behind! Do not say: "we don't know anyone" or "No one's asked." They are there, in your community, and in your pews. They are also silent, perhaps, to their peril.

Angie Fuoco

*"Love the Lord your God
with all your heart and
with all your soul
and with all your mind
and with all your strength.
The second is this:
Love your neighbor as Yourself."
There is no commandment greater than these.*

Mark 12:30-31 NIV

SECTION I
"BILL OF RIGHTS FOR THE HARD OF HEARING"

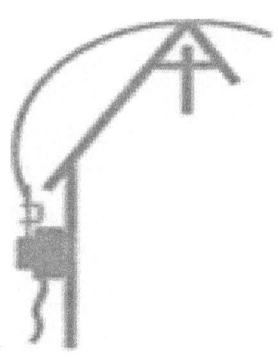

Bill of Rights for the Hard of Hearing

Hello, Can You Hear Me O.K?

I am profoundly hard of hearing and need you to face me, so I can read your lips.

You may be hard of hearing yourself or know someone who is struggling with hearing. You are wondering to yourself, "How do I deal with this issue?" and "Where can I get help?"

It is so exasperating when you have to repeat something over and over. You keep missing words and misunderstanding. It makes you angry when those hearing aids just don't pick up the missing words. "Why don't they work properly?" you say. The church is full of hard of hearing people, and little is being done to help them hear the Word of God.

They are embarrassed to speak up and ask for help. Many of hard of hearing drop out of the church and won't come back. Nobody knows what to do, so the church just ignores the problem and hoping it will go away.

Hearing loss is the fastest growing disability group in the country, due to loud music and I-pods that are on full volume. It is called self-inflicted hearing loss.

To challenge someone who has hearing loss

to get help, they will deny there is nothing wrong with their hearing. "It's your problem," they will say, "You mumble your words and don't speak clearly."

Pastors, teachers, speakers, and lay leader have no idea what to do. This book will give loads of tips, helps, and strategies that may make you and your loved ones happy.

The idea of the Bill of Rights for Hard of Hearing in the church is not legal laws to be obeyed; it is not a bunch of Do's and Don'ts. It is a demonstration of God's love to people with hearing loss.

The Bill of Rights for Hard of Hearing in the Church provides solutions and remedies for hearing problems

The hearing crowd may think that these ideas are rubbish and are a waste of time. Some are not willing to take the time to meet the hearing needs of their members.

The ideas must be put into practice if we are to preserve those who are still in the church.

A little love with kindness and understanding can go a long way. It is a simple method of including all hearing disabled. Not to practice this kind of love excludes those who want to be a part of the church and desire to hear the Word of God and enjoy fellowship.

We cannot continue to ignore our dear brothers and sisters in our midst. They are lonely and long to be a part of the church family. Your hearing matters to me and things are going to improve for the better. Talking louder is not a good idea of communication with a hard of hearing person.

Pastors have said to me, "We have one of those FM units for anyone who will ask for it, doesn't that take care everything?" It may surprise you, but I am hard of hearing in every other department in the church. I need hearing accessibility in all of these other areas.

When I pray to the Lord, I thank Him for your willingness to read the Bill of Rights for Hard of Hearing in the Church. Any application of one idea can be such an experience of love.

To hear in any other department can be such an encouragement. It will lift our spirit and the morale of the meeting. I feel better and at peace when I know you care.

This kind of love gives the feeling of inclusion and understanding so we can participate in the discussion. You gain confidence when fear of ridicule is minimized.

Dear Friend, I am asking you to be fully united in mind, heart, and attitude and read about this beautiful application of love. Don't be discouraged there are alternative methods and strategies that can improve communication skills greatly.

I am not here to tell you that the Bill of rights for hard of hearing is a magic formula that applies to everyone. It is an act of love that can do wonders for you and your loved one.

Jesus asked us to "Love your neighbor as yourself."

Do the Good Samaritan act and help someone in need.

Purchase an FM system

Begin your mission outreach to the hard of hearing; you will need to purchase an FM system that will do the job.

May I encourage you to get system that is versatile and durable? I have use Williams Sounds services for years. The hearing units have channels for language translation.

My recommendation is the PPA VP 37 Personal PA^R value pack system. Plan to have at least eight receiver units and include a special case for storing the units in.

Have the units visible so visitors can choose a unit. There are several types of earpieces to choose from for comfort. The units should be numbered for checkout and return purposes. Each person needs to sign in and check out upon return.

The display should be impressive and inviting for people to hear in the church service.

First Impressions of Your Church

You want visitors at your church and the way you welcome them may encourage them to come again. Some churches appear to be museums with little life. When your church becomes hearing accessible for hard of hearing, put enthusiasm into greeting a new visitor.

The *first impression* begins outside with signs announcing that the church is hearing accessible for hearing impaired. Promote on the marquee or a billboard. The announcement can be obvious and striking.

The parking lot needs to have special places for those who want hearing accessibility. Signs on each entrance door state that this church is hearing accessible. *Welcome!*

Inside the main door a visitor is greeted with a six-foot banner inviting him or her to visit the Hearing Center for an Assistive Listening Device (ALD). The sign over the center explains how the system works. Several types of earpieces and headsets are available.

The key to getting visitors to come back is within the four walls of your church. There needs to be genuine excitement and enthusiasm. Treat each visitor royally. Hard of hearing members should greet the visitor and share a testimony about the FM system.

Entering a church that is fully hearing accessible is a new experience. Prospects have heard about the hearing system and come to test it out.

Don't disappoint them.

Many hard of hearing have nowhere to go to hear the Word of God clearly. If they are happy, they will tell a family member and friends about the units. There is no need to drop out of church due to a hearing problem. We want to include you in every activity to the church.

Every person with hearing loss is looking for something special: love, kindness and fellowship. It does no good to spend thousands of dollars on advertising to get people to visit and give them a poor reception when they come through the door. We care about your hearing loss and want you to hear the Word of God clearly.

The Hearing Center

Setting up the hearing center is necessary. The FM system we use is from Williams Sound systems. The goal is to create an experience that will wow the visitor. We want them to receive extraordinary service. The initial service given on the first day may keep them coming back.

Hard of hearing people can be timid about visiting the church and trying out a hearing device. Give them confidence. They did the right thing about coming to church. A kind and loving spirit can win their heart.

When the visit to us is a positive experience, they will actively advocate the hearing center to others. It can be done by word of mouth and by literature. One or two willing members could help lead the church to growth and success. This is the ministry and mission of the hearing center. An experience you must hear for yourself.

The first thing you will see are the signs pointing to the hearing center. The case with the hearing units is neatly stored. Each unit is numbered, and the earpieces are close by. There is a belt clip on the back of the unit to put on your belt, in your pocket, or around your neck. Sign the checkout card for each unit so we know who has it. These units are not to be taken home.

Hearing Center Manager

Someone has to be at the center at all times for latecomers and for problems that may come up. Your job is to explain how the units work and remind them to return the unit to the center. If they are having technical problems, come to the center for another unit.

Maintenance of the units.
We want the units to be sanitized for use.

When the unit is returned, check for any defects. Use disinfectant wipes or alcohol swabs to clean the base of the unit. Headsets that have a sponge covering may be cleaned with a disinfectant spray. Hold the can about ten inches away from the earpiece and give it a puff. Do not soak the foam because it could damage the speaker unit inside. Let it dry and return it to the storage case.

You can get disposable covers for the earpiece in black or white. They are expensive. I found these covers to be durable and they can be washed and dried.

The earbud can be wrapped around the hearing units for storage. It is not recommended to purchase headsets from stores like Radio Shack. Most of the headsets have stereo jacks and do not work with a mono-socket receiver.

Registration forms

Every person who visits the hearing center should fill out a registration form.
1. Pick out a unit and earpiece (choice of earbud or head set).
2. Write your name on the sign out sheet along with the number on the unit.

3. The unit may come with a lanyard.
4. The unit must be returned to the hearing center.
5. It will be sanitized and serviced for your next visit
6. Do not take them home (They are useless outside the church).
7. We do have Tele-coil wire loops for those who have "T" switches in their hearing aids.
8. If you have any problem with the unit, come to the hearing center for replacement.

Role of the Pastor

All new visitors should be welcomed from the pulpit. The pastor should be the chief cheerleader and promoter of the FM system. You must become the biggest advocate and crusader from the pulpit. Give reports and testimonies of the blessings the hearing ministry has been to the hard of hearing community. Announce visitors who come and recognize them publicly.

The hard of hearing depend on their eyes and ears to understand the message. They need to see the pastor's face at all times, even when you pray. Always use the microphone under your chin so your voice can be heard through the FM listening system.

The key to getting visitors to come back is within the four walls of your church. There needs to be genuine excitement and enthusiasm. Treat each visitor royally. Hard of hearing members should greet the visitor and share a testimony about the FM system.

Entering a church that is fully hearing accessible is a new experience. Prospects have heard about the hearing system and come to test it out. Don't disappoint them.

Many hard of hearing have nowhere to go to hear the Word of God clearly. If they are happy, they will tell a family member and friends about the units. There is no need to drop out of church due to a hearing problem. We want to include you in every activity of the church.

Every person with hearing loss is looking for something special: love, kindness, and fellowship. It does no good to spend thousands of dollars on advertisement to get people to visit and give them a poor reception when they come through the door. We care about your hearing loss and want you to hear the Word of God clearly

The Role of Ushers

Ushers have a critical role in the dynamics of a hearing accessible church. Greet every visitor as a long-lost friend returned home. Hand out bulletins and ask if they need a hearing device. Ask every visitor to fill out a visitor's card to put in the offering plate.

It is imperative for ushers to be visible at all the entrances of the church during the main service. Visitors may come late and have no idea where to pick up a hearing device or where to take their children. Ushers can use a hearing device and not miss the service.

Deacons can patrol the parking lots to prevent vandalism. Each worker can have an FM unit and listen to the entire service. This can save you money, not having to hire a police officer. These workers can patrol the office and classroom areas if needed.

Classroom Accessibility

The teacher is the key to making the hard of hearing feel welcome in the classroom.

The classroom is a challenging setting for hard of hearing. The opening session of most classes begins with sharing what is going on in the community. Members of the class give out announcements and requests for prayer. As a person with hearing loss, I usually sit in the front of the classroom. All discussions take place behind me, and I have no clue who was speaking or what was said.

When the classroom becomes hearing accessible, teachers need to change the way the teaching is done. We need to be aware that there are hard of hearing members of the class all the time. Do not assume that because you have prepared the lesson everyone understands you perfectly.

Please be conscious of those present who have hearing loss, even if they don't admit it. It's embarrassing to be singled out because we can't hear everything.

My recommendation is to teach as if everyone in the class is hard of hearing. How do I do that?

- Teach facing the group at all times.
- Do not talk while writing on the board.
- Avoid having people reading passages from the Bible.
- Repeat all comments, questions, and jokes.
- Minimize noise outside the classroom.
- Don't play a recording or video without captioning.

- Refrain from having one person dominate the discussion.
- Teach with love and compassion.
- Whoever prays, have that person stand so we can read his lips.
- Remember, every class has someone with a hearing loss.
- Individuals with hearing loss do not want to be pointed out.

Everyone benefits when these guidelines are observed. Do this as unto the Lord that all may hear the Word of God clearly.

Prayer time in the church

Prayer time is a difficult moment for those who are deafened and suffer hearing loss. The custom is to bow our heads, close our eyes, and fold our hands. We remain in this rigid position until 'the Amen' is spoken.

This section is perhaps the most difficult part for the hearing people to accept. This method of praying needs to change for people with hearing loss to participate. When Jesus was in the Garden of Gethsemane, He asked his disciples to "Watch and pray." In other words, "keep your eyes open." This was for a different reason; He meant to watch for the enemy.

The hard of hearing and deaf need to pray with their eyes open. Why? To read the lips of the person praying, read the captioning, or see the sign interpreter. We hear with our eyes.

Whoever is praying should face the audience, keep his head up and hold the microphone on his chin. It is best to have the person whom the pastor calls on to pray, to come to the front.

This will make it easier to see and hear who is praying.

Asking an usher or deacon to pray for the offering with his head bowed and faced away from the people is discouraging for hard of hearing.

There is no biblical reason to ask the people to bow their heads with eyes closed and no one looking. This usually is done by a pastor or an evangelist when giving the invitation to make a decision. This order is repeated several times when some people do not bow during prayer.

Do we sin if we do not obey the order to close our eyes? Where did this idea come from and why? Did Jesus practice it?

When your church becomes hearing accessible for hard of hearing, please remember we need to see what you are saying.

Pastor, when you give an invitation during prayer time, and someone is looking at you, talk to him or her personally. "Do you need to come and make a decision?" "Do you need someone to pray with you?" "Come down to the front and let us help you." "We have men and women who will pray with you."

When you talk to that one who is looking, someone else with their heads bowed may think you are talking to them.

When you have hard of hearing people in your prayer meeting, you must make allowance for them to see and hear everyone in the group. If the group is small, I hook up my PKT amplifier with an extension cord, ask them to pray in the microphone with head up.

Each group needs to be trained how to accommodate your hearing needs and situation.

Make Special Events Hearing Accessible

Make all special events hearing accessible. Hard of hearing people will come to all the events put on by the church. To accommodate these events outside the main sanctuary, you can disconnect the transmitter from the sound booth and set it up in another room. Take the receivers and hand them out to those who want them.

Now we can hear everything that goes on in the fellowship hall, banquet hall, gym, movies, weddings, and funerals. This all can be worked out in advance for all hard of hearing friends. There is hope for all who attend any event held at the church.

I have taken my FM system to lecture halls and asked for permission to set up. One church I know uses the FM system for square dancing. There are smaller units for a single person with a hook-up to a special speaker.

There are portable FM units for bus tours or museum tours. These can be demonstrated at our office. These units are ideal for translating in different languages. Each tour guide system provides peace of mind; complete, portable, turnkey solutions that stand the test of time and are designed to meet ADA accessibility guidelines

Make the Music Hearing Accessible

Music can set the mood and spirit of the worship service. If you are using a hymnbook, announce the page number at least three times. Give the people time to find the page. If you are using the big screen that projects the words, this makes it easy to follow.

Some individuals with hearing loss find it difficult to understand words sung to music. This applies to solos, groups, and choirs. The words need to be provided one of several ways; on the overhead screen, in the bulletin, or on paper.

Instrumental music does not need the words provided.

We still want to see the faces of singers, but lip reading is hard because of dragging the vowels of some words.

Conduct an All-Church Accessible Workshop

The hearing loss ministry must begin with an all-church workshop. Every member should try to attend to know how this ministry works and why.

To buy an expensive FM system and install it and never promote that you have it is a waste of time. Several churches have had their hearing devices for years, and no one has asked for it. If somebody ask for a device, the church people will scramble to find it.

Do everything you can to promote the hearing units and the captioning when you have it. There is a way to get every member in the church to become an advocate for the hard of hearing ministry.

Give demonstrations regularly from the platform as a reminder that the system is still available. Every time I board an airplane, I get the speech on how to use the flotation seat and the oxygen mask, etc. I have pretty much memorized those talks. Remember that on every flight some new people have never flown before. You may have new people in every church service who do not know about the listening units or the hearing center. When everyone is informed, the mission of reaching the hard of hearing will succeed.

Advertise Your Accessible Ministry

The public may not understand the term Hearing Accessible Church. Following are suggested ways to word your promotion.

- Our message is now accessible for hard of hearing friends and family.
- We have accessibility for hard of hearing in the church sanctuary.
- Services are now accessible for hearing impaired.
- Our services are equipped to help hearing impaired.
- We invite hard of hearing to try our new FM listening system.
- Do you have a hearing loss? We are equipped to help hearing impaired.
- Don't let hearing loss keep you from church. We are wired for hearing impaired.
- Hard of hearing? Try our new assistive listening system.
- Can't hear well enough? Try our new FM system
- Tired of missing the message? We are equipped for hearing impaired.

Bill of Rights for the Hard of Hearing

- Don't stay away because you can't hear. Try our new hearing system.
- Do you suffer a hearing handicap? Try our new amplified hearing system.
- We care about hard of hearing friends and family. Try new listening system.
- Hear everything clearly with our new assistive listening system.
- Try our new personal sound system for hearing impaired.
- Difficulty hearing? Hear the preacher loud and clear with personal unit.
- Hear better with personal FM receivers.
- We provide hearing assistance for hard of hearing.
- With personal FM receivers, you can sit anywhere in our sanctuary.
- Wireless technology means hearing impaired can sit anywhere.
- Our personal radio system delivers the message right into your ear. Ask about it.
- Try our enhanced amplified personal listening devices for hard of hearing.

Keep informing the public that your hearing system is available. Include a statement on all literature: bulletins, news sheets and ads, tracts, letterheads, bill boards, and marquee. Encourage

members to spread the word to hard of hearing.
    Add to telephone answering machine. Create colorful fliers and distribute to households in area.

**EVERY CHURCH
HEARING ACCESSIBLE
EVERY MEMBER AN
ADVOCATE**

SECTION II
21 WAYS TO COMMUNICATE
WITH HARD OF HEARING

David M. Harrison

Prayer: The most powerful form of communication

This book and ministry was born in much prayer and fasting. I had reached the end of my life trying to communicate with people.

It was very depressive to think that there was no hope for me. When I turned seventy, there was nothing left for me to go on. It was a day of doom realizing that I was finished with society.

Depression is not what I wanted for the rest of my life. My last resort was to turn my life over to God and let Him direct my life for good. It was the best decision in my later years of my life.

On January 1, 2006, I was determined to hear from God. Prayer is the simplest form of communication, yet it is the last thing we think of. We may say little one-minute prayers, thinking we made a big hit with God.

We treat God like a slot machine, hoping to hit the jackpot of heaven on pennies.

The Creator of the universe demands my attention if I want Him to change the direction of my life. It was time to get serious with the Lord God in prayer and seek His will for my life.

To show that I wanted God to speak to me, I decided to go on fourteen days of prayer and fasting, seeking a solution for the rest of my life. God loves to answer prayer when you get serious with Him.

God answered with many blessings, miracles, and opportunities to serve as a missionary and hearing loss support specialist to hard of hearing. God showed me that the largest untapped mission field in the country is hearing-impaired people, not the Deaf, who speak only sign language.

One out of every five Americans suffers from mild to moderate hearing loss. This means that one out of every five church members is hard of hearing. They struggle to hear the Word of God as I did and feel frustrated about it.

The book on the "Bill of Rights for the Hard of Hearing" is based on ten years of much prayer and research, seeking and discovering ways to help people with hearing loss.

I love life more than ever before. The key is not more programs, more training, more technology, and more conferences, but more time in secret prayer with The Lord. The only expense is your time. Turn off the TV and discover the presence and joy that God wants to give.

In my frustration to find time to pray, I decided to give God equal time over a TV program. To make sure that I was able to do this, I made a sign: "Do you want power with God or entertainment?" This sign created my personal hour of power with God. I am now able to spend more time with Him than with the world. It is a decision you have to want to make. The rewards are phenomenal and eternal.

Jesus asks His disciples, "Could you not watch (and pray) for one hour?"

The Power of Prayer During the MRI Experience.

The day, November 3, 2016, arrived for me to be tested for my hearing at Vanderbilt University Hospital in Nashville, Tennessee. These tests were given to determine if I qualify for a Cochlear Implant.

The first series of testing was with an audiologist for four hours, listening to many little beeps, sounds, and words. Sound equipment was plugged into my ears and I heard my own voice in the right ear for the first time in my life. I was previously told that my right ear was dead, with no chance of hearing.

After lunch, I met with the surgeon and team who will perform the surgery for the implant. After reading the audiologist's report, the surgeon explained to us how to get ready for the implant.

Next were the MRI and CT scans. Blood work drawn, the needle was left in my arm for injection of dye for the MRI (Magnetic Resonance Imaging). The machine looked huge, with a small hole in the center. It looked ferocious and quite frightening.

I put on a hospital gown and laid down on the narrow table. Placing my head on a padded block, the nurse inserted ear plugs and then braced my head with wedges to keep me completely still. A mask was placed over my face and a blanket was placed on me to keep me warm. A call button was given to alert the nurse if I was in trouble. The nurse told me to lie very still.

My initial thought was, this would be a quiet, peaceful time for me to pray for the next forty-five minutes. The table or bed was raised up and began to slide into the hole or chamber. Fear gripped me, and I felt claustrophobic; nausea made me feel like vomiting. I tried to quote the twenty-third Psalm to calm my soul.

Suddenly, a bright light came on followed by extremely loud noises: rumbling, grinding, banging, like I was inside a cement mixer full of gravel. The noise escalated to the level of a jet engine, a rushing subway train, sirens, hailstorm, and jackhammer all at once.

This mass distraction made it impossible to think, meditate, or pray. The intensity of noise overwhelmed me. Horror gripped me as I remembered that I must endure this for forty-five minutes. It felt like eternity. This might be what Hell may sound like.

I found it too difficult to quote the twenty-third Psalm, so I tried to sing out loud. Next, I decided to pray out loud with the intensity and urgency of a desperate person. I tried to get a message to God by shouting random prayers, but could God hear me in all this ruckus? Soon I felt a surge of power and peace, a sense of calmness in the midst of such chaos.

I recalled that most Christians would not pray for three minutes in a peaceful place, let alone any chaotic situation. We find many excuses for not praying and have lost our will to come boldly before God with our petitions. Something happened to me in those forty-five minutes that gave me a new perspective on prayer. It is possible to pray for an hour if you desire for God to bless you, regardless of the distraction.

"O Lord hear; O Lord, forgive; O Lord, give heed and act; delay not, for thy own sake, O my God, because thy city and thy people are called by thy name." Daniel 9:16

The CapTel Captioned Telephone

People with some degree of hearing loss need assistance to communicate on the telephone. The Captioned Telephone, or CapTel phone, works like any other telephone except you can read the words of the person you are talking with on a lighted screen.

This service is free to those who are hard of hearing. Fill out an application and have it authorized by hearing aid distributor, ENT doctor or audiologist. There is no charge for the phone, installation or service.

CapTel phones work with a Captioning Service as part of a federally funded program that supports telephone accessibility for people with hearing loss. No cost for the Captioning Service is passed on to consumers – no monthly fees, no service agreements. Your monthly phone bill does not change.

24/7 Help Line

We are here to help around the clock. With one-touch access to CapTel's knowledgeable customer support team, help is available 24 hours a day, seven days a week.

David M. Harrison

Spanish or English

You dial the other person's number, the same way as with any other telephone. As you dial, the phone automatically connects to a free captioning service. When the other party answers, you hear everything they say – just like a traditional call. The captioning service transcribes everything they say into captions so that you can read it.

With CapTel, you do not have to dial a toll-free number to access the service.

Your screen may be as big as 6" by 9" depending on the phone selected. Fonts can be enlarged for readability. You may get up to fifteen lines of texts at a time. The CapTel can store up to 480 lines of text. You can review the conversation after you hang up. You cannot print out text for future reference.

Answering Machine messages are captioned for you to read later. Voiced messages can be listened at that time.

The CapTel phone must be connected to high-speed internet service. The phone has volume control to help you to hear the message or speaker. You can use a headset or Telecoil neck loop to transmit sound into your hearing aid.

Calls are made and received over the telephone line, while the captioning service connects automatically through the Internet.

How does it work? Think of a triangle of three people.

1. Grandma is hard of hearing and has a CapTel telephone.
2. A grandson calls to invite her to a birthday party
3. Grandmas' phone rings and she answers.
4. The grandson says, "Hi Grandma, this is Bobby."
5. Bobby's voice is relayed to a captioned telephone operator.
6. She transcribes Bobby's words into text using voice-recognition technology.
7. Those words appear on Grandma's caption telephone screen.
8. Grandma is listening to Bobby's voice while reading the captions of what he is saying. The operator is invisible, and you do not know she is there.

For more information on the CapTel phone contact:

Sign up for a free no cost CapTel phone. **www.captel.com/**

If you have difficulty hearing on the phone, you may qualify for a no-cost CapTel phone. We will contact you to answer questions and help explain the certification process through your doctor or audiologist.

REQUIREMENTS:
- Difficulty hearing on the phone
- High-speed Internet access
- Home telephone service
- Signed certification from doctor/audiologist
- Most local audiologists may have the application to get your free CapTel Phone.

WebCapTel Captioning on Your Computer

Now you can have your phone captioning on your desktop computer or laptop. Use your landline or cell phone. Any computer Macintosh or Windows-based PC compatible or telephone will work.

Clear captioning depends on your browser window and font style. You can review and save the entire conversation on your computer. The text can be printed out for study. You will need to register at sprintcaptel.com

Per recent FCC regulations, individuals with hearing loss may receive an

Internet-based CapTel phone free of charge if they complete and submit a Third-Party Certification of Eligibility. The Third-Party Certification must be signed by a hearing health professional who confirms that the person applying has a hearing loss and would benefit from IP-based Captioned Telephone Service to communicate effectively over the phone.

Bill of Rights for the Hard of Hearing

There is no software needed to download to use Hamilton CapTel for PC/Mac?

Hamilton CapTel for PC/Mac is a web-based service and is activated through your Internet browser.

Anyone who has access to an Internet-enabled computer can register for a Hamilton CapTel Account and use Hamilton CapTel for PC/Mac service anywhere, anytime!

You can also log into Hamilton CapTel for PC/Mac to place and receive captioned calls.

Communication on the telephone is now effortless for individuals with hearing loss! **Sprint CapTel** has the latest technology and a dedicated team of experts to empower once again you make and receive calls with confidence. Can a phone change your life? Maybe it can.

Sprint WebCapTel is a web-based service that lets you read word-for-word transcriptions of your calls on a computer monitor or laptop. You can listen to your caller speaking through any telephone, including cordless, landlines or cell phones.

So, whether you are waiting for your state-of-the-art CapTel phone to be delivered or you aren't at home and need to make a quick call, use Sprint WebCapTel!

David M. Harrison

Clear captioning

ClearCaptions FREE Web Service Provides Real-time Captions to Any Phone. Add real-time captions to any phone in your home with

ClearCaptions Web, the online phone captions service, which captions your calls directly on your computer or laptop.

Near real-time accurate captioning displayed directly on your computer screen. Once the call is over, save the captioned conversation to review later. Easy to use and only requires an active phone line and internet connection. Change font sizes, font color and even the background color.

Braille Captioned Telephone Hard of Hearing and Blind to Hearing

We now have caption for the blind. This unit is ideal for braille readers who have difficulty hearing over the phone. The CapTel 880iB Captioned Telephone works like any other telephone with one important addition: it provides braille captions of

Bill of Rights for the Hard of Hearing

every word the caller says throughout the conversation. CapTel 880iB users can listen to the caller and read braille captions on their dynamic braille display reader.

The braille-captioned telephone is easy to use. Just connect your braille display reader to the Cap Tel phone. It works the same way you would use any other telephone. If you cannot hear what someone says, read the captions on your braille display.

Free Service

CapTel works with a free Captioning Service to transcribe everything the other person says into written words. There are no monthly fees or service agreements.

Your monthly phone bill does not change.

http://www.captel.com/braille/what-is-braille-captel/

Questions about Braille CapTel Services? Please contact: Braille@CapTel.com

Ultratec, Inc. 450 Science Drive Madison, WI 53711

Phone: 1-800-482-2424 V/TTY Fax: 608-238-3008

http://www.captel.com/braille/

David M. Harrison

Cell Phone Captioning

The demand for captioning is on the rise

Place and receive captioned calls on a single device with our unique and innovative app for iPhone and Android™ smartphones at no cost.[1] Hamilton CapTel is compatible with the latest smartphones[2] and tablets, on most wireless networks.

Don't have a smartphone? See every word a caller says on your iPad or Android tablet when using the mobile app in Hamilton CapTel for Smartphones allows you to read captions of what is being said during phone conversations while you listen and talk with people on the go! Similar to captions on a television, word-for-word captions of your conversation are displayed on your smartphone.

Place and receive calls on your mobile device and read captions of what is being said. You will never miss a word again.

The Hamilton CapTel® App is designed exclusively for individuals who have difficulty hearing over the telephone. With this app, you may listen to your phone conversations while reading word-for-word captions of what's said to you - similar to captions on TV.

This app update includes compatibility with

cell phones: Hamilton CapTel Call Me #.

To receive calls, you must have a Call Me #. Log into your account at www.HamiltonCapTel.com/login to obtain your Call Me # today!

Learn more about Call Me # and how it works, visit:

www.HamiltonCapTel.com/callme
Video: https://vimeo.com/190619819

Use your iPad or Android Tablet with any telephone (i.e., landline, office, mobile phone) to place calls with the Hamilton CapTel App. Captions of what is said appear on the tablet screen while you listen and talk using your desired telephone.

Register for a Hamilton CapTel account to ensure your mobile captioned calls are placed securely and accurately. This simple, one- me process will allow you to place and receive captioned calls any me you are logged in with Hamilton CapTel. You download and install the Hamilton CapTel App, simply enter your Hamilton CapTel account information and you will be ready to make and receive calls immediately.

The Hamilton CapTel Call Me # is one simple, smart solution for all your smart devices.

The Hamilton CapTel Call Me # is your phone number that makes it possible to receive captioned calls on your computer, Smartphone, and Tablet. Share your Hamilton CapTel Call Me # with family, friends, and businesses and answer your next call with captions on the smart device of your choice.

Get your Hamilton CapTel Call Me # today! Simply log into your Hamilton CapTel account, visit "Receive Calls" and click on the Call Me # link. It is that easy. Also, your Hamilton CapTel Call Me # is free!

Web and mobile CapTel services, which include without limitation, Hamilton

CapTel Service ("Hamilton CapTel for PC/Mac" or "Hamilton CapTel for Smartphones" or "Hamilton CapTel for Tablets") handle 911 calling differently than traditional telephone services.

Using traditional telephone services is the fastest way to call 911, as your telephone, TTY or CapTel phone provide a direct link to your emergency service provider. In contrast, web and mobile CapTel services do not provide a direct link, so it is important that you provide your location information to the 911 center at the beginning of the call to transmit your physical location to an emergency center.

Sorenson videophone (deaf to deaf in ASL only)

The Sorenson Videophone was specifically designed for deaf-to-deaf communication. Sign language only.

The Sorenson Videophone works through a high-speed internet connection.

It is a specialized unit that works like a telephone, but does not have sound, only pictures of the caller and the receiver.

The videophone allows you to make calls to other deaf who have a videophone receptive unit.

These units have an exclusive dialing system to connect you to a deaf person. Each party speaks sign language to each other without an interpreter in between.

The videophones have a call-waiting feature to let you know you have another call coming in on the other line. You can answer the call and go back to the original caller.

Should you receive a call on your videophone and no one answers, the caller can leave a message, like a recorder, but a video recorder and leave a message in sign language to watch later.

Another amazing thing is that you can conduct a conference call with The Group Call Feature. As many as four (4) parties with videophones can talk at the same time. You can also make a second call while the first party is waiting for you to come back.

Each videophone unit has a large TV screen with a high definition camera mounted on top. The unit is modified for the communication network supported by a Wi-Fi connection to your internet router.

Deaf cannot hear the phone ring. In order to get the attention of the recipient, there is a high-powered strobe lighting unit installed. It is called LightRing" to alert the deaf party a call is coming in. The lights are three times brighter and come in colors that identifies the caller.

The best part I like is you can give a personal greeting when the call is not answered. You give a "SignMail" greeting in ASL and then ask the caller to leave a signed message.

www.sorenson.com

Sorenson Video Relay Service

Created for the Deaf to communicate with the hearing world. An exclusive development by Sorenson to bridge the gap between Deaf and the hearing.

When a Deaf person wants to place a call to a hearing person, he/she presses the quick-call button on the Videophone for the operator. This number also reaches customer service and technical support.

The operator answers and converses with the Deaf in Sign Language in English or Spanish.

The caller gives instructions to dial up a hearing person's number and ask for a specific by name.

When the hearing person answers on a standard phone, the relay operator will voice the name of the Deaf person who is calling. The operator gives a message, and the response is relayed back to the Deaf person.

The relay operators are trained, professional interpreters. They will relay the Deaf person's Sign Language to a verbal message to the hearing.

Sorenson offers extensive services, technical support, and educational videos so the Deaf can communicate with anyone, anywhere, at any time. When a hearing person wants to connect with a Deaf person the concept reverses. Using a standard phone or cell phone, he dials the number of the Deaf person directly.

This call is routed through an interpreting center, where the operator will answer for the Deaf. The videophone will light up with special strobe lights to alert the Deaf that a call is coming in.

These calls take a little extra time. Be

patient. Every call is important and is worth the effort. When you are talking, speak as if you are talking to the Deaf person directly even though you are hearing the operator's voice.

When you speak, the operator will relay your message to the Deaf in Sign Language. You will hear the message verbally from the Deaf.

Each person is speaking in his or her native language. How cool is that?
This service is offered 24/7 and is paid for by the governments Telecommunication's Relay Service (TRS) fund. Contact Sorenson.com or www.sorensonvrs.com

AVA Deaf Person to a Hearing Group

In 2016 Cathy and I attended the International Federation for Hard of Hearing in Washington D.C. At the end of the conference, we were invited to see a demonstration on a new hearing accessible product. Four young men from Europe showed how captioning can be done on a cell phone. Since then the group has changed the world of communication with hard of hearing and Deaf.

Permission given to copy information

A letter from Thibault Duchemin

Ava is an application for the Deaf and hard-of-hearing people to empower them to understand

& participate in-group conversations by showing them in real time who says what.

Our system swiftly pairs smartphones in a room and processes the conversation to show you, the deaf person, and a real-time, color-coded transcript of the discussion.

At business meetings, family dinners or social gatherings, you launch the app, and Ava does the rest. Ava is transforming communications for the deaf/hard-of-hearing people by bridging communication gaps with a 24/7 personal, lightning fast, and affordable captioning experience.

In a group situation, every hearing person is asked to key in a "AVA ID" code. Each of these phones becomes the microphone for a captionist to translate or caption the message on the cell phone of a hard of hearing or Deaf person.

The hard of hearing or Deaf person can follow the conversation of every person in the group. Each speaker is identified by name. Don't miss out in group conversations anymore. Share your unique **"AvaID"** link with others so they can join your conversation on their Ava app. At lunch, in meetings or hanging out with friends, Ava shows you who says what, in real time, and in colors.

Connect quickly one or multiple friends, next to you or at any event anywhere in the world. It takes one tap to connect you all.

Join the other Ava Pioneers exploring every day new ways to use Ava to make the world more accessible. Ava 1.0 is just the first step towards a 24/7 accessible world. Visit www.ava.me/life for more details on how other Pioneers use Ava.

Experience the first artificial intelligence designed to empower deaf & hard-of-hearing people. Anyone can tap on words that Ava got wrong to teach her. Ava gets smarter at understanding you & your peers' voice.

Bringing the deaf & hearing worlds closer, one conversation at a time

Today, we're excited to announce the launch of Ava on iOS & Android. Ava turns smartphones in a room into smart microphones, allowing the deaf/hard-of-hearing person to read the entire conversation as real-time captions- including who said what.

It started with an immense frustration

We started Ava in 2016 out of an immense frustration: those we loved and millions of deaf & hard-of-hearing people like they were being confronted with the difficulty of following a "simple" group conversation, every single day. Participating in groups is a right evident to those who can hear—but not for over 400 million hard of hearing people in the today.

I grew up the only hearing kid in a deaf

family. With Skinner, himself deaf, and Pieter who taught himself sign language, we thought that there ought to be a better way for all the moments where a $100 an hour professional interpreter or captionist is not an option. A viable way to make accessibility affordable, anytime, anywhere.

Hearing, deaf and hard-of-hearing people of the world: Ava is an app you need to have on your phone.

Together, let's build a more accessible world. *The Ava Team,*

Bridging the communication gaps between deaf/hard-of-hearing & hearing people. Ava captions conversations in real-time. 24/7 accessible: all you need is a phone.

We are bringing the deaf & hearing worlds closer, one conversation at a time.

Find all of the latest Ava news on our Twitter account @avascribe or our Facebook page: facebook.com/avadotme Video: https://vimeo.com190619819

https://vimeo.com/190619819

We are together because we deeply believe that hundreds of millions of deaf & hard-of-hearing people in the world should have the right to live an accessible life. By total, we mean total: accessibility should be possible anytime, anywhere, for everyone.

David M. Harrison

The wall of silence can break; it must! While we know it will not be easy, our journey from the last two years led us to think that this future, while extremely ambitious and uncertain, is possible. A slight chance: that is all we need to work hard to beat the odds.

Hearing aids work well enough in many cases but often fall short in group conversations. The distance between participants and the background noise around them makes it harder for a hearing aid to do the job.

The dynamics of a group conversation mean that you lose the *visual* accessibility component because reading lips is *much harder*. Hearing aids are often not sufficient, and part of the problem is that most people do not realize this!

Developing innovative speech recognition technologies with the expertise in the accessibility issues is the only way to get to the radical cost decrease that is needed. It is an extremely hard problem, and that is why Ava is a technology company at its core.

At Ava, we are from many walks of life and cultures. Experiencing the deaf/hearing communication gap frustrated us so much that we decided to try to do something about it.

Awareness is the way to go forward. If we are just a technology company, we will not be able to push forward the impact we ought to make. As a social enterprise, it is our responsibility to go beyond, to be more. For you, and all the others.

UBI Duo 2

The UbiDuo 2 communication device, cuts through all the clutter of technology, without computers, or internet Wi-Fi hook up. No need for telephones or making contact with the cell phone or waiting for someone to come and interpret in Sign Language.

With the UbiDuo 2 communication device, the conversation is instantaneous while typing to each other. Communication is done in real time. No need to hit the return key to send out a response. Just sit down and type out your conversation. It becomes a genuine face to face conversation allowing each other to see their conversations in real time while watching each other's facial responses and body language.

This unit was designed for deaf, hard of hearing or people with voice problems where they cannot speak. This opens up a completely new field for handicapped and disabled people.

The next generation UbiDuo 2 text to speech

(TTS) is now available. We are talking about face to face technology, the world's first communication device with real-time, split-screen text, and dual text to speech for people who are deaf, hard of hearing, late deafened, hearing and others with communication disorders.

This is the ultimate instant communication solution allows two people to communicate in real time using text, text to speech, and both at the same time.

Now you can have a technical discussion with your doctor, boss, co-worker, professor, and teacher for detailed information. There is no warm-up period or electrical hook-up to get started. You no longer have to call and make an appointment with an interpreter and wait for them to show up. It is not the same as captioning which makes mistakes. It not limited to texting where you send a message and wait for a reply.

It is the world's foremost solution for people who need help with communication. The UbiDuo unit is a portable tool you can carry with you at all times. It is rechargeable with a Micro USB port for charging. You can download all your discussions on a USB type flash drive. It has the capability of connecting to a HDMI port for TV or Projector.

Would not you like to be able to have a non-stop communication conversation in your environment every day at home, the hospital, university, agency, or at work?

HUMAN INTERACTION IS THE ESSENCE OF LIFE

Interact, communicate, and be everywhere.

The UBIDUO units are not cheap. They range from $2000.00 to almost $4000.00. Many college campuses have them in the disabilities office for students to use.

The optimum for everyone, deaf, hard of hearing, and hearing, is to be able to experience barrier-free, communication without interruption when they choose at any time 24 hours a day, 7 days a week, 365 days a year. You do not need to pay $100.00 per hour for a captionist or for an ASL interpreter.

The UbiDuo 2 speech Generating Device (SGD) is covered by Medicare/Medicaid and private insurance. We can help you navigate through the process to secure coverage for the UbiDuo 2 SGD by guiding you through the easy steps and completion of required documents. One of our Communication Access Advisors who is either hearing or deaf will be assigned to your case and you be able to count on their knowledge and experience to work with you and take you through every step to the way.

The UbiDuo 2 is a stand-alone device that

facilitates direct face-to-face communication, which means the deaf and hearing person can sit across from each other and communicate in a natural flow through real time text. The UbiDuo 2 empowers deaf or hard-of-hearing individuals and hearing individuals to converse face-to-face from one to as many encounters a day as they desire even up to 100% of the time.

It does not matter whether you are in a family setting, on a business trip, or trying to talk with a co-worker "communaphobia" is a real fear. The UbiDuo can eliminate this fear and help bring together relationships of deaf and hearing people in any setting, anywhere at any time.

We want to give everyone 100% one-on-one communication equality. We are passionate about liberating people who are deaf, hard of hearing, and hearing from faking their way through conversations and getting frustrated about what was said.

Our passion leads us to create the best face-to-face communication technology to give rich and invigorating conversation experiences for people who are deaf and hearing.

The UbiDuo helps people interact with each other and share their professional and personal lives' most meaningful experiences. The way a moment of barrier-free face-to-face conversation with another person is more meaningful than being isolated.

Sharing our collective experiences makes our lives richer and more fun.

For more information contact:
www.sComm.com
> 6238 Hadley Street
> Raytown, MO 64133
> 866-505-7008 (Toll Free)
> 816-737-1790 (Fax)
> 866-505-7001 (TTY Toll Free)
> 816-527-9079 (Videophone)

TTY Relay Phone Calls

Since the invention of the telephone, hearing-impaired people were unable to communicate by phone. For generations, deaf and hard of hearing people had to depend on hearing family members, friends, and neighbors to make telephone calls for them.

Robert Weitbrecht, a deaf scientist, developed the teletypewriter (TTY) in the 1960s. With the invention of the unique coupler to hold the telephone handset receiver and the distribution of recycled teletype machines, deaf and hard of hearing people were able to call each other directly using these devices.

TTY stands for Text Telephone. It is also called a TDD, or Telecommunication Device for the

Deaf.

People who are not deaf also use TTYs.

A TTY is a special device, which allows deaf to type messages back and forth to one another instead of talking and listening. A TTY is required at both ends of the conversation to communicate.

If you do not have a TTY, you can still call a person who is deaf, hard of hearing, or speech-impaired by using the Telecommunications Relay Service (TRS). With TRS, a special operator types whatever you say so that the person you are calling can read your words on his or her TTY display. He or she will type back a response, which the TRS operator will read aloud for you to hear over the phone. Toll-free TRS services are available 24 hours a day, 365 days a year.

State and federal programs provide this service free to people who are deaf, hard-of-hearing, deaf-blind, and speech-disabled.

Calls can be made to anywhere in the world, 24 hours a day, 365 days a year with no restrictions on the number, length, or type of calls. All calls are strictly confidential and no records of any conversations.

Deaf leaders established the National Association of Deaf (NAD) in 1880. They believed in the right of the American deaf community to use sign language, to congregate on issues important to them, and to have its interests represented at the national level. These beliefs remain true to this day.

Early achievements by the NAD, such as securing the right to federal civil service employment and the right to drive a car, are overshadowed by the continuing and constant struggle for equal access and equal opportunities to education, employment, health care, and justice.

Finger Spelling (Manual Alphabet)

Sometimes simple things can help us communicate with a hard of hearing or Deaf persons. As children, we received manual alphabet cards. We would play with them but never took them as a serious means of communication.

Now that I am writing twenty-one ways to communicate without hearing aids, finger spelling had to be on my list.

A Franciscan Monk, Melchor Yebra, created alphabet or finger spelling before sign language. His finger spelling letters were picked up by Laurent Clerc to teach deaf children in Paris. In 1817, Thomas Gallaudet introduced the method of finger spelling to children in his Deaf Institute in Hartford, Connecticut. The school later moved to Washington DC.

Finger spelling is best used between family

members or friends for clarity.

You do not have to learn signs for specific words, just spell them.

The Rochester Method of finger spelling is used only to supplement speech and lip reading. We must speak or form every word on our lips at the same instant we spell it.

When you type, you automatically type the words without spelling them.

Your fingers do the spelling, while you think or say the words. This is the way finger spelling works.

Start with the proper position for finger spelling. Are you ready? Raise your right hand or left hand, please. Your hand is facing out at your chin level. Try this, place your left hand under your right elbow. That is the correct position for elbow and hand. Do not bounce your letters up and down for emphasis but keep it in a steady position. The only thing that moves is your fingers.

Say the words and spell with your fingers slowly. Practice slow, clear spelling and then increase your speed after you have set good spelling habits.

Keep in mind you do not need to spell every word you speak.

You will need to spell names, streets, titles of book or movies for clarification. Always spell out technical, legal or medical terms for clarity.

Groups of Deaf people have used sign languages through history. Until the 19th century, most of what we know about historical sign languages is limited to the manual alphabets that were invented to transfer words from a spoken to a signed language. *(History of Sign Language - Wikipedia.)*

In 1620, Juan Pablo Bonet published "reduction of letters and art for teaching mute people to speak" in Madrid. It is the first modern treatise of sign language phonetic, setting out a method of oral education for deaf people and manual alphabet.

Finger Spelling is an important part in our need to communicate when no other method will work.

The only thing you need to learn is the twenty-six letters of the alphabet and ten numbers. Do not try to spell all the words in a sentence. As you speak, spell keywords that may be helpful. Mouth the word silently as you fingerspell.

Start a game with a family member to practice daily with the alphabet and simple words. Never give up on this method. It is the cheapest non-technical means of communication with hard of hearing. It does not cost anything to start but a little of your time to learn and practice.

Hearing aid users and those with cochlear

implants need special help to clarify words that are difficult to understand. No matter how much you paid for a hearing aid, you still miss words. Hearing aids do not restore hearing to perfection. Clarity gets lost in the most expensive technology occasionally.

Learning the finger spelling alphabet can be overwhelming. Children can pick it up fast when it is in fun. The shapes of the letters are used in American Sign Language. This game has progressive speeds that can that you increase as you progress. It begins with three-letter words, then four letters and up to five letters.
https://www.handspeak.com/spell/practice/

American Sign Language

American Sign Language is a form of sign language developed in the US and used in English-speaking parts of Canada.
American Sign Language (ASL) is a visual language. With signing, the brain processes linguistic information through the eyes. The shape, placement, and movement of the hands, as well as facial expressions and body movements, all play important parts in conveying information.

Sign language is not a universal language — each country has its sign language, and regions have dialects, much like the many languages spoken all over the world. Like any spoken language, ASL is a language with its own unique rules of grammar and syntax. Like all languages, ASL is a living language that grows and changes over time.

Many high schools, colleges, and universities in fulfillment of modern and "foreign" language academic degree requirements accept ASL across the United States.

Throughout its history, the National Association of Deaf (NAD) has celebrated achievements that have improved the quality of life for people who are deaf or hard of hearing. The advocacy efforts of the NAD, including those led by the NAD Law and Advocacy Center, continue as new challenges arise.

Here you will find a wide range of

information for deaf and hard of hearing individuals, their families, and friends. This information is also helpful for employers, businesses, and government agencies seeking to provide equal opportunity and equal access for individuals who are deaf or hard of hearing.[1]

Total Communication

(TC) is an approach to Deaf education that aims to make use of some modes of communication such as signed, oral, auditory, and written and visual aids, depending on the particular needs and abilities of the person.

Simultaneous communication,

SimCom, or sign supported speech (SSS) is a technique sometimes used by deaf, hard-of-hearing or hearing sign language users in which both a spoken language and a manual variant of that language (such as English and manually coded English) are used simultaneously.

Body language and facial expressions and other forms of communication may enhance manual communication when it is a primary form of communication. Manual communication is employed in sign languages and in systems that are codes for oral languages.

Expressive vs. Receptive Communication

Expressive Communication is when you are sending a message; this may be in response to another person or to initiate communication. Receptive communication is when you receive a message from another person. An individual's expressive and receptive communication skills may not be the same. People will use a combination of the communication methods listed above, both expressively and receptively. For example, a person may receive and understand information in sign language and need symbols to help reinforce the meaning but will use sign language and speech to express themselves.

The total communication approach values all methods of communication by connecting differently.

Manually Coded English

(MCE) is a variety of visual communication methods expressed through the hands, which attempt to represent the English language.

A contact sign language, or contact sign, is a variety or style of language that arises from contact between a deaf sign language and an oral language (or the written or manually coded form of the oral language).

Manually coded languages are not themselves languages but are representations of oral languages in a gestural-visual form; that is, signed versions of oral languages (signed languages). Unlike the sign languages that have evolved naturally in Deaf communities, which have distinct spatial structures, these manual codes (MCL) are the conscious invention of deaf and hearing educators, and mostly follow the grammar of the oral language — or, more precisely, of the written form of the oral language. They have been mainly used in deaf education to "represent English on the hands" and by sign language interpreters in K-12 schools.[2]

We all communicate differently, and some of the specific methods for communicating with people with multi-sensory impairments require special training and experience.

P.S. There are books, classes, and videos everywhere to learn American Sign Language.

Lipreading

Lipreading is a language for hard of hearing. Lip reading is a language all its own. How can that be? If American Sign Language is the second language for the Deaf, then lip reading is the second language for the hard of hearing.

Both are a part of the natural language for disabled people.

As "seeing ears" are the eyes to the blind, so "hearing eyes" are the ears for the hard of hearing. The eyes become the third ear for the hard of hearing and ears become the third eye for the blind.

Lip reading takes the English language to a higher level through visualization of words. You already know the language; now you will learn it from the visual point of view.

The speaking voice moves dozens of muscles per second for each sound spoken. The average person does not think of all the movements that go into producing a word or a sentence.

We will analyze the various movements for sounds and show each person how to teach him/herself the art of lip reading. There are some simple techniques to make this happen.

With more than 50 million Americans who suffer mild to moderate hearing loss, they should consider lip reading to augment communication skills. Few colleges in America offers lip reading as an alternative to sign language. Most hard of hearing people do not want to learn signs because there no one available to speak with them.

Lip reading can be used anywhere, anytime, with anyone in any language. It is important to understand that lip reading needs to be done within close range to be effective.

What captioning is to TV and movies, so lip reading is to the hard of hearing. These four components to lip reading can improve your communication skills.

First is what you see with your eyes: facial and lip movements and expressions. There are body language and animation of the speaker.

The second part is what you hear. 98% of people with deafness are hearing impaired, in other words, they have some residual hearing. These people depend on some amplification such as hearing aid, pocket amplifier, wire loop system, infra-red or FM listening system.

The sad part is that most people are not aware of any technical devices to improve their communication ability.[3] The third component of communication deals with techniques and strategies. Whether you have a hearing aid or not, you can improve your hearing by much as 30%. The Lip Reading Academy presents some simple methods that can enhance any one's hearing ability. The ideas can be applied easily as soon as you understand them.

The fourth component seems the most precarious. When all the above fail, then you can take chances and guess what you may have missed. This method can cause many problems and breakdowns in communication. Making a mistake in what you thought you heard can cause arguments, fights, and hurt feelings.

There is a solution to this method. Tell others that you have a hearing loss and did not understand the message or word spoken. Ask them to repeat what was said and thank them for their help.

Lip reading, also known as speech reading, is a technique of understanding speech by visually interpreting the movements of the ***lips***, face, and tongue when normal sound is not available,[4] also relying on information provided by the context, knowledge of the language, and any residual hearing.

Lip reading allows you to "listen" to a speaker by watching the speaker's face to figure out their speech patterns, movements, gestures, and expressions.[5] The greater the hearing loss, the more a person tends to rely on vision in order to understand speech. Benjamin Franklin said, "When you speak to another person look them in the eye when the other person speaks, look him in the mouth."

Lip reading is facial linguistics in which the grammar of movements of the body and face helps to understand the spoken language. It does not work well with musicals where words are sung.

When a person is unable to communicate in

a group situation, he tends to withdraw from social situations and go into seclusion away from the public.

Sign language (or simply signing) is a language which uses manual communication and body language to convey meaning, as opposed to acoustically conveyed sound patterns. ASL can involve simultaneously combining hand shapes, orientation and movement of the hands, arms or body, and facial expressions to fluidly express a speaker's thoughts.[6]

Learning American Sign is not for the Deaf who want to speak with other Deaf. They already know the language. Learning lip reading is not mainly for hearing people, but for those who have hearing loss, so they can converse and communicate with the hearing world. It does not make sense for Deaf to take classes in ASL.

The hearing loss people of America need to learn a second language to improve communication, a language that enhances his mother tongue and one that can be assimilated into his natural speech pattern without effort. Lip reading is now the second language of most people with hearing loss.

No longer will we accept a third language imposed by the Deaf.

It is time to make a distinction between people with hearing loss and those who are deaf. They are not in the same language bracket or category. Deaf interpreters are few and far between. Lip Reading is the second language of the hearing impaired and is everywhere.

Cued Speech of London

Cued Speech is a complete spoken language through vision. The first time I heard about Cued Speech was through a membership of the Royal Institute of National Deafness (RIND) of London, England. I had entertained the idea of going to the Cued speech training Institute.

Cued Speech can be learned by hearing parents and teachers in only 20 hours. It can transform the lives of deaf children by giving them complete access to spoken language in real time. They can then develop an understanding of English, which will give them access to the language of hearing family members and the wider community.

In 2016 Cathy and I attended the cued speech training at Camp Cheerio located in the beautiful Blue Ridge Mountains of North Carolina. It was a family camp with board, lodging, and recreational activities for all ages.

I was surprised that Cued Speech was taught in the U.S. Very little is known about the organization in America. The National Cued Speech

Association is based in Washington, D.C.

Cued Speech is a simple and extremely cost-effective system of cues; eight handshapes in four positions near the mouth together with normal speech, which clarify lipreading.

Cued Speech makes the spoken language visible to all ages of Deaf. English without barriers is their motto.

Only 35% of speech can be accurately lipread. With Cued Speech, the accuracy of the language rises to 96%. This full understanding of English (or other spoken languages) leads to high literacy levels.

Cued Speech is not exclusive; it can be used to supplement the use of hearing aids and implants, or it can be used bilingually with British or American Sign Language. It is used with other spoken languages and in many different countries.

Cued Speech has been adapted into 60 languages and dialects so far and was devised by the late Dr. Orin Cornett, Professor Emeritus of Audiology, Gallaudet University, USA.

The Cued Speech Association UK (CSAUK) is a registered charity run by users of Cued Speech (both parents and professionals) who provide information about and training in Cued Speech.

National Cued Speech Association
1300 Pennsylvania Avenue, NW Suite 190-713

Washington, DC 20004
1-800-459-3529 http://www.cuedspedspeech.org
www.cuedspeech.co.uk

Captioning in Public Places

Captioning may be necessary and required to make audio and audiovisual information and communication accessible to people who are deaf or hard of hearing in a wide range of situations.

Many public entities have obligations under civil rights laws or American Disabilities Act (ADA) that prohibit discrimination and require the provision of accommodations, such as captioning, to ensure equal access, an equal opportunity to participate, and effective communication with people who are deaf or hard of hearing. [7]

Captioning in Churches:

Every church has a pocket of people who suffer hearing loss and would benefit greatly from captioning in the main sanctuary. The FM system is not always perfect but supplements the spoken word from the pulpit.

A captionist can bring captioning remotely from anywhere in the country. Using a Skype program, the sermon can be printed on the big screen in the church. The sermon is printed out on paper and sent to the pastor within forty-eight hours.

Read more about the multiple uses we can benefit from caption later on in this book.

Captioning in the Classroom

Colleges are required to provide captioning for the disabled students. The professor can be hooked up on a laptop camera with Skype. The captionist is watching the lecture and sending back the caption. Students can log into the Skype on his cell phone or laptop. The notes can be downloaded on his computer for later review.

Type Well Captioning

The term captioning refers to the very thing a <u>Type Well</u> transcriber does: types out what people say so that hard of hearing can have communication access to the message.

The terms transcription, transcriber, and transcribing are used in place of the words caption, captionist, and captioning. There are two main reasons:

The text of the federal Americans with Disabilities Act uses the term "computer-aided transcription services" to refer to equal communication access services, and the term "captioning" is used to refer to the text translation at the bottom of TV broadcasts, movies, and videos.

There is widespread popular understanding of the word "captioning" to mean this "text below a picture." In fact, the Individuals with Disabilities Education Act uses the term "captioning" in exactly this way, and not to refer to in-class communication access and notes.

Thus, transcribing is the more accurate term to refer to the communication access, and notes mentioned in the federal laws, and using the term transcribing avoids confusion of these two access services with the other, very important access service of "on-screen" text: captioning.[8]

Automatic Speech Recognition

Automatic c speech recognition (ASR) defined as the independent, computer driven transcription of spoken language into readable text in real me (Stuckless, 1994).

Briefly, ASR is technology that allows a computer to identify the words that a person speaks into a microphone or telephone and convert it to written text.

Having a machine to understand fluently spoken speech has driven speech research for more than 50 years. Although ASR technology is not yet at the point where machines understand all speech, in any acoustic environment, or by any person, it is used on a day-to-day basis in some applications and services.

The ultimate goal of ASR research is to allow a computer to recognize in real- me, with 100% accuracy, all words that are intelligibly spoken by any person, independent of vocabulary size, noise, speaker characteristics or accent. Today, if the system is trained to learn an individual speaker's voice, then much larger vocabularies are possible, and accuracy can be greater than 90%.[9]

Classroom Captioning

Remote CART Services — Real- me text services that allow hard-of-hearing and deaf students to read what is being said in the classroom. Pu

ng true real- me remote CART services, or classroom captioning, in place for your hard-of-hearing and deaf students will provide a cost-effective and useful service.

While interpreters, note takers, and print services provide a condensed version of what is said in a class or lecture setting, CART provides the most comprehensive and complete translation for your students. Remote CART is not intrusive, meaning the student only needs to have their computer available for the service instead of a live CART writer or interpreter. This also allows easier movement from class to class for the student.[10]

Captioning in Worship Service

With increasing demand from congregations' elderly and hard-of-hearing memberships for CC as a part of their worship experience, knowledge of captioning and how to move forward with it is becoming an essential component of the video production knowledge base. "Tapping into closed captioning, and getting it right, is more important to religious, corporate and even online entities than ever before," Philip McLaughlin concludes. "For houses of worship, closed captioning is a strong reinforcement to their message at many, many levels."

For more information on Captioning go to the back of book

Texting

Once we had to stamp and mail letters to far-flung friends and family members. Nowadays, written messages can be instantly delivered thanks to texting – also known as **short messaging service**, or SMS –and **instant messaging**, or IM. Both give you the ability to directly communicate with your contacts, but texting and instant messaging have differences that may make one a better option for you.

There are so many different ways to send text messages today, that regardless of whether you use an iPhone or an Android. You may have heard of different acronyms like SMS and MMS.

SMS stands for **Short Message Service**. Invented in the 1980s and defined in the 1985 GSM standards, it is one of the oldest texting technologies. It is also the most widespread and frequently used.

MMS stands for **Multimedia Messaging Service**. It was built using the same technology as SMS to allow SMS users to send multimedia content. Its most popularly used to send pictures. Standard SMS messages are limited to 160 characters per message. Unlike SMS; MMS messages do not have a standard limit.

SMS is a universal technology supported by every single mobile network and device today. All you need to start texting over SMS is another person's phone number. This makes SMS a popular channel for businesses to communicate with customers because it is more immediate than email and does not require any additional app downloads.

SMS is most popular in the US since most

carriers offer plans with unlimited texting, making SMS free or nearly free to use. Texting has exploded over the last decade to the point where we are currently witnessing over 6 billion SMS messages sent daily in the US alone. Annual MMS traffic in the US increased from 57 billion to 96 billion messages from 2010 to 2013. With no significant costs to hold them back, we are seeing US smartphone owners aged 18 to 24 send an average of 67 texts a day.

People are spending a significant amount of time on their phones these days: the average American adult uses a mobile device nearly 3 hours every day. Since much of this time is spent texting, many businesses have correctly surmised that SMS is one of the most effective channels for businesses to reach new and existing customers.

People simply prefer to communicate with businesses by text. The higher open and response rates — 90% of all text messages are read within 30 seconds — make SMS marketing even more attractive, especially when used in the context of customer service.

Text messaging from your cell phone is a quick and easy way to stay in touch. Anyone can learn how to send a text message on a cell phone with practice and some patience. Eventually, sending a text message can feel as natural as sending an e-mail or talking on the phone. [11]

You can select the Microphone icon near the keyboard on the iPhone to send a **voice-activated message**. After you select this icon, speak the message you would like to send as clearly as possible. The phone will not add punctuation to the message, but this is an effective way to send messages if you cannot or do not want to type.

Watch your manners and tone of voice when texting. Say thank you and please. Show a little love and appreciation.

You can now send text messages from your computer.

Combine your recipient's 10-digit phone number with one of these domains:

- Alltel: @message.alltel.com (or @mms.alltelwireless.com for picture messages)
- AT&T: @text.att.net.
- Sprint: @messaging.sprintpcs.com.
- T-Mobile: @tmomail.net.
- Verizon: @vtext.com (or @vzwpix.com for photos and video)

WARNING—WARNING – WARNING
Read carefully

Organizations and individuals are called upon to urge those they care about to:

Stop using cell phones while driving. Understand the dangers of the cognitive distraction to the brain Inform people who call you while driving that you'd be happy to continue the conversation once they have reached their destination

Tell others about the dangers of cell phone distracted driving[12]. Half of all teens will be involved in a car crash before graduating from high school. Parental involvement does not end when a child gets a license. Teen drivers who continue to practice with their parents increase their chances of avoiding a crash.[13]

The digital era has certainly ushered in exceptional innovation. You can connect with anyone, anywhere in the world with a few simple clicks. Mobile messenger platforms like Facebook Messenger and WhatsApp make it easy for teens to stay connected with friends and family at all times.

However, this has made the smartphone another accessory teens simply cannot live without. When was the last time you saw your teen without their smartphone more than an arm's length away?

Smartphone ownership and use by teens is commonplace. According to eMarketer, 87 percent of teens aged 14 to 18 years old owned a smartphone.

The reason texting while driving is so dangerous is that three major physical and mental actions are happening at once. Texting draws a teen's attention from the road, and the potential dangers ahead.

Texting causes these distractions while driving:

Cognitive Distraction: Your teen will no longer be mindful of the main action, which is driving due to the need to grab, use, and process communication to and from those texting them.

Visual Distraction: When your teen driver takes his or her eyes from the road to read or type a text message, their visual attention is no longer focused on the road.

Manual Distraction: To grab for a phone and most likely type in or swipe a security password to access their phone, your driver's hands are no longer on the wheel. This causes a lack of control over the vehicle.

Brain activity is reduced by 37% when using a cell phone while driving.

The NHTSA report stated, "For these distraction-affected crashes, the police crash report stated that the driver was talking on, listening to, or otherwise manipulating a cell phone (or other cell phone activity) at the time of the crash. A total of

476 people died in fatal crashes that involved the use of cell phones or other cell-phone-related activities as distractions."

It would be safe to say that teen drivers, in combination with cell phones, is a recipe for disaster. Chimes of incoming calls and texts, texting while driving, and even hands-free calling can be potentially deadly.

The National Safety Council says that mobile phone use now is the leading cause of death behind the wheel. Texting causes one out every four car accidents. Eleven teenagers die every day while texting.

Regardless of how smart your phone is, we need smarter drivers.

The highway sign says: "One Text, one call, can end it all."

Skype

What is Skype?

Skype is a free video-chat software application that works similarly to instant messaging. You download the software and build your list of contacts; when they are online, you can call and talk to them for free. This enables users to make free phone calls to other countries through their computer for free.

This works out great for businesses that are working as teams from various parts of the country or world, for professionals that have international business dealings, communicating with family in other countries or members of the military stationed overseas. The sound quality is great, and all you need is a headset.

There are currently more than 521 million user accounts registered with Skype. However, the downside to Skype's genius is people were tethered to their computers. Skype was never designed to replace your home phone, but to merely use your computer as a tool to supplement the capabilities your phone lacked. To counter this, Skype introduced SkypeIn, SkypeOut and eventually Skype Pro.

SkypeIn

SkypeIn is a paid service where people that do not have Skype can call you from a traditional phone. Skype provides you with a traditional phone number that you can give to your friends and family, and they can call you just like normal.

However, for their calls to reach you, you have to be on your computer and signed into your Skype account.

The beauty of this feature is if you live in a

different country, but your family is in the United States you can request a local U.S. phone number as your SkypeIn Virtual Number and their calls to you would not cost anything more than a local call.

SkypeOut

SkypeOut is also a paid service that gives you, the Skype subscriber, the ability to make phone calls to traditional landlines using your

Skype software. You can also call cell phones for about 2.1 cents per minute. SkypeOut also charges a connection fee for less than a dollar to most industrialized countries.

Skype in the future

Skype is very popular, and its popularity is only growing around the world, especially in Europe where the software was originally developed. In early

2008, Skype joined with Sony to incorporate the software into the PSP Slim & Lite handheld gaming device. Using a wireless connection and Skype, you can use your personal skype phone (PSP) like a phone.

Skype and other VoIP services have gotten off to a slow start, but as highspeed Internet becomes standard and the digital age takes off, they are going to become the standard, and traditional phone lines just might be going dead.

http://www.toptenreviews.com/services/articles/skype-explained/ Skype is an IP telephony service provider that offers free calling between subscribers and low-cost calling to people who do not use the service. In addition to standard telephone calls, Skype enables file transfers, texting, video chat and video conferencing. The service is available for desktop computers, notebook and tablet computers and other mobile devices, including mobile phones. Some companies, including Skype, produce dedicated Skype phones.

Note Taking

When I meet a Deaf man on the street, he may show a card that he is Deaf and needs money. If I ask him a question, he produces a piece of paper to explain his situation.

Writing a message is difficult to read or understand. We try hard to get our messages across to each other. In most cases, I can give the Deaf man a few dollars for his cause.

I know a sweet couple where the husband lost his hearing and ability of speech. They attended Sign Language training but did not do well with it.

Later they came to our Lip Reading classes, but it did not work out for them.

The wife carried a legal pad with her all the time and was constantly writing messages to him. His responses were in writing on the same pad. She was very patient with him and never complained.

While attending college I learned, I could get help. Following a lecture in the classroom that was too difficult for me so, I went to the disabilities office and asked for help. The disabilities office hired a student to attend the classes or someone within the class to take notes. This has been very helpful in my studies. The note taker is paid for attending the class and gives me a copy of the notes.

Another time, a student typed the lecture notes on her laptop using large fonts for me to read. It was not the same as captioning but was helpful.

"Lip Speaking"

What is lip speaking?

A lip speaker is a hearing person trained to repeat a speaker's message to lip readers accurately, without using their voice. They produce the shape of words, the flow, rhythm, and phrasing of natural speech and repeat the stress as used by the speaker. The lip speaker also uses facial expression, natural gesture, and finger spelling (if requested) to aid the lip reader's understanding.

Messages, which are too fast for lipreading,

may have to be pared down by the lip speaker, who is not more than a sentence behind the speaker. Many people speak up to 200 words a minute; lip speaking, therefore, requires a high level of concentration. If two people speak at the same time, neither message can be passed on.

Lip Speaking Is Not the Same as Lip Sync

Lip sync (short for lip synchronization) is a technical term for matching a speaking or singing person's lip movements with prerecorded sung or spoken vocals that listeners hear, either through the sound reinforcement system in a live performance or via television, computer or cinema speakers in other cases. The term can refer to any of some different techniques and processes, in the context of live performances and audiovisual recordings.

Who uses lip speakers?

Lip speakers are mainly used by deaf, deafened and hard of hearing people who use lipreading as their first means of communication with other people. These lip readers generally have good English skills. Hearing people may use a lip speaker to communicate with deaf people. A lip speaker may be employed to aid communication between lip readers and hearing people in a range of situations

I have used lip speakers on several occasions where I could not see the speaker's face.

While attending a deaf meeting where someone was speaking out of my sight or off stage. I signaled to a sign language person to mouth the words of the speaker.

I could hear the speaker's voice, but not clear enough for to distinguish the words. With the help of the lip speaker made a big difference in comprehension of the message.

My sign language is not good enough for me to grasp fully what the speaker was talking about. I depend heavily on lip reading, even with hearing aids. It is important to try as many different methods of communication as possible. Every day I meet new challenges in unusual places.

Professional lip speakers are popular in the United Kingdom. It is helpful when a doctor or dentist is wearing a mask and talking at the same time. I am profoundly hard of hearing and without my hearing aids; I am deaf. It is very thoughtful if someone is mouthing the words of the doctor.

E-mail

Multi-part address where the first part (the user name) identifies a unique user. The '@' separates the user name from the host name which uniquely identifies the mail server. The three-letter suffix following a period (dot) identifies the kind of organization operating the mail server. Addresses outside the US use another (two-letter) suffix that identifies the country where the mail server is located. By convention, all email addresses are typed in lower-case (common letters) without any spaces separating the different parts.

Read more: http://www.businessdictionary.com/definition/electronicmail-address.htm

A means or system for transmitting messages electronically (as between computers on a network) communicating by e-mail. Electronic mail (email) is a digital mechanism for exchanging messages through Internet or intranet communication platforms.

Techopedia explains *Electronic Mail (Email)*

Email messages are relayed through email servers, which are provided by all Internet service providers (ISP). Emails are transmitted between two dedicated server folders: sender and recipient. A sender saves, sends or forwards email messages, whereas a recipient reads or downloads emails by accessing an email server.

Email messages are comprised of three components, as follows:

- Message envelope: Describes the email's electronic format
- Message header: Includes sender/recipient information and email subject line

- Message body: Includes text, image, and file attachments

Short for electronic mail, e-mail or email is information stored on a computer that is exchanged between two users over telecommunications. More plainly, e-mail is a message that may contain text, files, images, or other attachments sent through a network to a specified individual or group of individuals.

The first e-mail was sent by Ray Tomlinson in 1971. Tomlinson sent the e-mail to himself as a test e-mail message, containing the text "something like QWERTYUIOP." However, despite sending the email to himself, the e-mail message was still transmitted through ARPANET.

Hospital Communication Board

A visualized-based Empower Communication Board can support those with limited to no speech in a clinical or hospital setting.

It is very important that patients in the hospital be able to inform the nurses and staff their personal needs. Research has shown that this type of board can improve patient satisfaction, reduce frustration, and improve patient outcomes

This amazing Empower Communication Board is a compact 8" x 14", which unfolds into a self-contained stand for easy viewing.

The Empower Communication Board (ECB) is frontline healthcare communication. It enables individuals with communication challenges to participate in and direct their care throughout a medical encounter. The ECB offers multiple overlay designs based on research to suit the cognitive, linguistic, and motor needs of the individual. It can be used as a single overlay to gain attention or answer yes/no/I don't know questions. The board merges into a combination of overlays that can be used to deliver a more complex message.

The entire board is laminated and can be used as a convenient dry-erase surface that allows the patient or listener to write or draw items to ensure messages are understood.

Research supports the use of video modeling techniques to train communication partners. Attainment is excited to offer staff, families, and friends the opportunity to access an easy-to-use video tutorial via a QR code on the ECB. The video provides quick training at bedside as needed.

There are seven ways to communicate with patients to express their needs.

1. Emergency Response Overlay: Offers useful

vocabulary for basic, early communication in times of waking from sedation.

2. Category Overlays: Presents overlays in a hierarchy of need. As the patient becomes more alert and his or her communication needs expand, more categories can be used. This area of the board is accessed when symbols are needed to decrease demand for literacy skills, provide context, as well as allow for communication on various topics. The food tab can be flipped over out of view if eating is not an option.

3. Text overlay: Allow for creation of novel utterances. The focus is on the acute inpatient setting.

4. ABC Keyboard: Displays keyboard with highlighted vowels presented at first for ease of partner assisted scanning if necessary. Vocabulary for repairing or managing message creation is available.

5. Pain Scale Overlay: Offers the traditional 1-10 pain scale choices.

6. Pain Script Overlay: Provides communication options for patient caregiver to work through a painful event.

7. Dry-Erase Overlay: Appears as a blank page the patient or communication partner can use this to write novel utterances, draw messages, or to provide a visual cue when giving verbal directions. Includes Training Video:

David M. Harrison

http://player.attainmentcompany.com/empower/

Section III

My Seed Dream

My SEED dream is to MEET the invisible NEED of
a disability not SEEN but one we all FEEL and
BLEED emotionally and
REEL from the impact of it
HEARING LOSS
The DEED of my heart and the CREED of my soul
is to HEED the call of GOD
and KNEEL to His leading with KEEN obedience
to GOD to
FEED those who long to hear
It is my DEEP burning desire to REDEEM the time
to KEEP striving with GOD
and STEER the dream to reality
LET MY PEOPLE HEAR!
David M. Harrison copyright 2009

David M. Harrison

Before I Die Campaign

In the year 2006 the Lord directed me to begin a unique ministry to reach out to the multitude of hard of hearing people inside and outside the church. My quest began by taking academic studies to prepare me to serve as a hearing loss support specialist. This specialized training certified me to become a missionary advocate for hearing accessibility in the church.

Recently, we attended a senior networking meeting in Coolidge Park to see a special display. There was a portable chalkboard wall (8' x 40') called "Before I Die."

Mr. Gary Mac, an advocate for Hospice, explained the purpose of the wall

"Before I Die." Dying patients would write their dying wish of doing something noble. It was discovered when dying patients put their wish or hope on a worthy cause in writing, they live longer. They became committed to make their wish happen.

We were challenged to write our final wish before we die. It has been my prayer to reach out to Hard of Hearing people and the churches. This has been my strong burden and passion since 2006. I knew what my calling and ministry has been these past ten years. I wrote this on the wall: Before I die.

> **"I want to see scores of churches become fully hearing accessible for hard of hearing in every department."**

In my heart I wanted to write 10,000 churches in my lifetime. My dream can be accomplished by publishing the book: **The Bill of Rights for Hard of Hearing** in the church. This book is a demonstration of love to reach out to the hearing impaired in and outside the church.

Every hard of hearing person can now inspire and challenge the church to become hearing accessible. Every pastor, missionary, and teacher must see the hard of hearing as a mission field.

We must stop ignoring our members who suffer hearing loss. It is a serious problem that should be addressed in every church. Do not let this hearing accessible mission die. We need your help.

Revival can begin when we pay special attention to a specific need of a group of people.

American Disabilities Act

Does the church discriminate against people with hearing loss? Often, I see a sign or hear a statement like: "American Sign Language is provided for deaf and hard of hearing."

I cringe when I see this because ninety-five

percent (95%) of all hearing-impaired people do not know sign language. Our need for communication is different from the 5% who are deaf.

My wife and I were visiting a church when I told an usher that I was hard of hearing. Instantly he said, "There is a person here that knows sign language." It is assumed that persons with any level of hearing loss speak sign language. Not so! My request was for an FM listening device.

The American Disabilities Act (ADA) of 1990 established a series of measures to prohibit situations of discrimination because of a person's disability. The ADA law requires that the communication needs of hard of hearing and deaf be provided with such reasonable accommodations. For the hard of hearing, it means providing an FM or a telecoils loop hearing system.

The law states:

"No individual shall be discriminated against on the basis of disability in the full and equal enjoyment of the goods, services, facilities, privileges, advantages, or any place of public: by any person who owns, leases, or operates a place of public accommodation."

The law continues discrimination to include: *"Failure to take such as may be necessary to ensure that no individual with a disability is excluded, denied services, segregated or otherwise treated differently than other individuals because of the absence of auxiliary aids and services..."*

Any place of public gathering is required to provide effective means of communication for hard of hearing individuals. According to ADA standards, it is up to the institution to pay for any reasonable accommodations. If an institution does not comply by providing a hearing system for hard of hearing individuals, it may suffer serious penalties.

Providing access to an assistive listening system is not only the law, but it's the right thing to do. It includes hearing disabled people and helps them feel part of the fellowship.

Hearing loss is the largest disability covered under the ADA. Nearly 20% of every congregation has members that need assistive listening units.

Why don't they come out and say something? There are two reasons:

1. Hard of hearing people do not know what is available to help them hear better. They have trouble hearing but don't want to speak up for fear of embarrassment. They may not be aware of any other person who has a hearing need. Some hard of hearing friends drift to the back of the church. It does not take long for them to begin skipping church and Bible hour. The reason some of them stay in the church is because of their family. Believe me; they are not getting much out of the service or

Bible teaching.

2. Hearing people do not know how to help those with hearing loss. The only thing that comes up is to turn up the volume and talk louder. In most cases, yelling only distorts words and makes it difficult to distinguish sounds. Many times, there are jokes about people with hearing loss. Family members may nag them about getting their ears checked.

Hearing accessibility must be taught to the entire congregation, not just a few individuals. Why is this so important to the local church?

In the USA alone, there are some 50 million Americans who have a measurable degree of hearing loss. These people make up the single largest disability group, equaling one out of every five adults. Churches may not have to comply with the ADA, but it is the right thing to do.

WARNING: This is not a legal document. If you are having trouble getting proper accommodations for hearing, please talk with a lawyer who understands the ADA law.

The ramp for the hard of hearing is not made of wood and steel but of love and kindness to Accommodate their need to communicate.

The ADA public facilities include the workplace to provide reasonable accommodation for people with disabilities. This meant every public building should have wheelchair ramps, handicap bathrooms, and elevators as well as Braille signs for the blind and handicap parking spaces.

The ADA is a civil rights law designed to prevent discrimination and enable individuals with disabilities to participate fully in all aspects of society. This ruling declares that anyone who is qualified to perform a job must have an equal opportunity to work. The act includes the Deaf and the hard of hearing.

The hard of hearing are a unique group of people who have their own set of needs different from those who are socially and culturally deaf. The Deaf depend entirely on American Sign Language, whereas the hard of hearing may not use sign language but depend on assistive listening devices (ALD) and other means of communication.

Of the 50 million deafened Americans, only 500,000 are culturally deaf and speak ASL. The hard of hearing community continue to struggle to communicate with little help or assistance.

The hard of hearing group of people is the largest disabled group in the world and is growing larger every day. You can find them in every family, social group, classroom, office, place of business and in every church.

The general public cannot cope with the idea of people who are severely, moderately or mildly hard of hearing, yet hearing loss is one of the most common impairments that inflict the human race.

We have seniors over fifty-five who are losing their hearing due to the aging process. They talk and hear, but not everything. Many wear hearing aids and still misunderstand words spoken.

It is extremely difficult for me as a hard of hearing person to pick up on a rapid group conversation, I miss the punch line of most jokes, and fall behind over idioms and play-on words. I am the only one wondering what was said while everyone else is laughing. No one wants to repeat the punch line, or they will tell me later. When this happens, I feel isolated and rejected from the group.

The hard of hearing have special needs that must be addressed if they are to communicate in the hearing world.

The World Health Organization (WHO) explains deafness and hearing impairment. "There are two types of hearing impairment, defined according to where problem the occurs:

a. Conductive hearing impairment, which is a problem in the outer or middle ear. This type of hearing problem is often medically or surgically treatable if there is access to the necessary services; childhood middle ear infection is the most common example.

b. Sensorineural hearing impairment, which is due to a problem with the inner ear, and occasionally with the ear the hearing nerve going from there to the brain. This type of hearing problem is usually permanent and requires rehabilitation, such as lip reading, strategies dealing with coping and use of hearing aids.

What is hearing accessibility?

There are two parts of hearing accessibility. The first part deals with all the technology that is placed into the sound system. This includes an FM listening device, a telecoil loop unit for those who have a T-coil in their hearing aids, and a hard-wired unit hooked up to the PA or the infrared light system and another host of other electronic inventions. In spite of all the big loudspeakers placed around the sanctuary, this is not the complete answer to accessibility.

Please note that hearing aids are not the definitive answer to hearing accessibility. They are only an aid, not a cure. You still need a method to assist you with communications.

Technology in communication is only 10% of accessibility and strategy is 90%. The second part deals with methods or strategies of communication. We must connect with the hearing loss needs of each. In the heart of every hearing-impaired person is a burning desire to distinguish and understand sounds, speech, warning signals, and words sung to music. Every group that starts a discussion becomes difficult to follow. Background noise and many voices create a hodge-podge of noise.

Church members suffer the most because the church is not intended to minister to hard of hearing. It is not easy to explain why it is so difficult to hear and understand what is going on. The largest part of church activities is outside the central sanctuary where all the technology is. Now we must find alternative ways to enhance communication. Some of these activities may include the fellowship hall, gymnasium, conference room, prayer meetings, and Bible studies.

The list of places of hearing difficulty intensifies in the work community, hospitals, theaters, restaurants, and shopping malls.

Many companies will sell technology for a price and call it accessibility. Most of these items are limited to one room or place for services. We are hard of hearing in every area and department of the church where there is no technology.

Where can we go to find a church that is exclusively accessible for the hearing handicap? There is no such place in existence.

My greatest desire is to be able to function and participate in every meeting and service in the house of God. It is humiliating to miss much of what is said and not be able to respond correctly. I became determined to do something about the situation.

My purpose is to create a total hearing accessible church for people with hearing loss. This set up would become the testing ground for various methods of accessibility. This unique building will become the forerunner of the future for churches to follow and ideas for the general public to consider and adapt.

We will have a situation room that will become the testing ground to experiment with ways to better communicate with those who suffer hearing loss. It will be a place to create and develop a better hearing center. It will be a laboratory for new ideas.

It is urgent that we establish an advisory team to lay the groundwork for new ideas. My prayer is that talented men and women will join the team to design and create a magnificent, functional place.

Impairment of hearing can hit you at the very core of your being because it limits your ability to communicate with others. You enter into a lonely communication vacuum from the hearing world when you cannot hear. You feel like you are the only one in the world with this problem.

In the Bible, Elijah was running from the enemy and hiding in a cave. He cried to God and said,

"I am the only righteous person left." God responded, "Elijah, you are not the only one left, there are 7000 righteous persons like you on the other side of the mountain."

You are not the only one that has a hearing problem and needs help; there are fifty million plus Americans like you that need some assistive help hearing. Hearing loss is serious because it cannot be repaired or restored to normal.

You isolate yourself from your family, your social life, place of business, and from your church family. The only thing you can do now is to pray that God would intervene and help you overcome this problem. It seems so depressing to cope. You search desperately for understanding and support of your disability. You long for someone who may have the same problem communicating as you do to come and comfort you.

The purpose of the bill of rights or guide to hearing accessibility is to encourage people to change the way we communicate with each other. This book is like a game plan that you learn and put into practice.

If you are going to go on a diet, you will want to research the best program to follow and adopt it. Many adjustments need to be completed if you want to succeed. First of all, you will change the way you eat. Second, you stop eating certain foods and increase other healthy choice foods. Third, you must follow the guidelines rigidly and religiously. Fourth, there are exercises.

Every program ventured involves the entire family.

It is not easy to break old habits. It is even harder to learn new habits that could benefit you greatly. We must be on guard at all times and resist every temptation not to follow the guidelines. In the end, the new way becomes the norm, and everyone is happy.

These principles apply to just about everything we do in life: learning a new language, playing an instrument, and preparing for the Olympics. It all begins with a need and then it becomes a burning desire. We must study and research a new idea until it turns into a plan of action. You commit yourself to work the plan and practice it daily without fail.

A well thought out plan can be very productive. (Proverbs 21:5) I must continue working with the hearing impaired. It has become a passion with me.

A Hearing Accessible Church

The largest disability group in America is the hard of hearing group. They are not deaf or know sign language. They do have individual communication needs.

One out of every five Americans has a hearing loss. That means that every church in America has a pocket of hard of hearing people.

Going to church now becomes a struggle for those with a mild hearing loss even when wearing a hearing aid. Understanding the message becomes confusing as well as the music, Bible study, and the prayer time. They suffer alone in silence.

Rather than face these trials in trying to hear the Word of God, it seems easier to drop out and not attend church anymore.

Hearing loss is the most common physical impairment among the human race, yet the most misunderstood disability. We do not know how to deal with the kinds of behavior that occur with hearing loss. It not only impacts behavior but affects relationships. Some hard of hearing people may be implicated of being slow or senile.

It is easier for the church to overlook this problem rather than try to ease the situation.

If we are ever going to reach the vast population of hard of hearing outside the church with the Gospel, we must first prepare to meet their physical need to hear.

It would be wonderful if the church realized that we have a primary disability group among our members. It would be very thoughtful if something could be done to meet this great need.

The international symbol for hearing accessibility has a cross on top to indicate that the church should become accessible for all hard of hearing.

Let's make the church hearing friendly for the hard of hearing. In most cases, the sanctuary is already wired for accessibility. Now we need to work on the other areas in the church. Our aspiration drives us to create a place where every hard of hearing person can function and understand what is going on in all activities of the church.

When the church becomes more hearing accessible, then I can personally, along, with others become more active in the total ministry of the church. With all those who suffer a loss of hearing, I would be willing to participate more without fear of embarrassment or intimidation.

Communication Gap Syndrome

Every day I struggle with a Communication Gap Syndrome© or disorder, a major handicap for any hard of hearing person. When information is missing or unclear, it affects the language learning process, both receptively and expressively. Everything becomes muddled and incomprehensible.

Between what you say and what I hear, there

is a great gulf fixed. If you think your hearing loss is not a problem, what about all the words you misunderstand? There is a gap between your speaking and my hearing. Your message in my ears sometimes is full of gaps.

The gap syndrome takes place when a number of people are in a discussion that merges into a jumble and becomes a communication nightmare. The words I miss cause misunderstanding of the whole context of a conversation. Getting accurate information can be difficult.

The gap syndrome appears many times a day: at home, work, school, neighbors, and church. Every social activity continues to create more problems. Getting directions from the TV, radio and telephone is a pain. Do not ask me if you miss a word, to set you straight.

Jason Curry, who invented the UbiDuo created the word "communiphobia" for the fear of missing out in a conversation. He describes when a deaf person and a hearing person meet and do not know how to communicate with each other. The deaf person does not hear or read lips and the hearing person does not know Sign Language. All they can do is smile and move on.

They may resort to writing notes to each other for some basic information. They cannot carry on a good conversation of any depth.

I think of a beautiful puzzle with some key pieces missing or an important document with some key words blanked out with a marker. The full meaning is missing.

The goal of this book is to bridge the gap, making sure that you will understand and hear more than you miss. We call it communication accessibility access by breaking down the barriers to conversations.

There are strategies and technologies that will help minimize the gaps in your life. We may not get to all of them, but every little bit can improve your peace of mind.

Hang in there and do not give up. Help is on the way. Try out any of the methods in this book that you are comfortable with and stick with it.

Never stop learning or trying new ideas of communication. Have fun and others will help you. Stevenson said, "Keep your fears to yourself, but share your courage."

Defensive Hearing for Communication

Hearing loss is a pandemic-like health issue spreading like wildfire. We all depend on our hearing to stay in touch with our world of friends. Hearing loss separates us due to miscommunication.

Educators, leaders, and coaches need to

seriously consider the long-term effect of how hearing loss impairs a person's ability to understand spoken language.

What is the defensive hearing program for hard of hearing?

Let me illustrate with the concept of "defensive driving." Every new driver is advised to attend a program to understand how to survive driving on the road. It not about what type of vehicle you drive but equipping the person behind the wheel.

The defensive Hearing idea works the same way. Hard of hearing people of any age can be referred to take a training program dealing with hearing loss. Whether you wear a hearing aid or not, defensive hearing can make a dramatic change in your life.

Hearing loss is forever. With a mild hearing loss, a person can miss up to 50% of a normal conversation, as well as what goes on in the classroom, on TV, a DVD or radio. Our goal is to prepare hard of hearing to face the world defensively with special training and strategy to function in the hearing world.

To practice defensive hearing is to struggle for better hearing. Defensive hearing for hard of hearing was developed after seven years of trial and error. While teaching lip reading to scores of people, I needed a word that would be helpful to people. The thought of defensive driving came to me. It is understood that we need to learn how to face traffic and drive-by protecting ourselves and avoiding accidents. It is not telling others how to drive around us but doing everything to make driving a pleasure and safe for us and others.

Defensive hearing is a program developed by Let My People Hear, Inc. intended to prepare hard of hearing to survive in our hearing world. It is protecting everyone from the stigma of hearing loss. The program is designed to help hard of hearing avoid pitfalls of miscommunication and threats to our ego and self-esteem.

No one wants to confess that he/she has a hearing loss, but everyone else knows they have it. There is a passive defense of struggling to cover up hearing loss with excuses or more denial. This may be practiced by pretending to understand when you have no clue what is being said.

We have to come up with an alternative method of hearing or communication, a method outside the box of the medical or technological field. We were looking for a procedure easy enough to put into practice personally. We have not yet discovered all there is to assist our hard of hearing friends.

David M. Harrison

Five Gates to Better Hearing

1. The Ear Gate - What you hear is extremely important. Concentrate on what you hear. Focus on everything that is going on around you. Take nothing for granted. Hearing aids can be deceptive due to limited quality. Ambient noises can muddle the speech sounds to make it difficult to get it right.

Analyze everything that is coming into the ear gate. Make sure you are on the same track with the speaker.

2. The Eye Gate -When I was taking Drivers' Ed, my teacher told me that I was very observant about everything that was going on. I watched every vehicle on the road to make sure we did not collide. To this day, I have never had an accident or been stopped by the police.

Your communication is enhanced by what you see. Lip reading, body language, facial expressions, and gestures are all part of the visual communication. Look into the eyes of the speaker and note what you see in your peripheral vision. You have to stare at the speaker if you want to get the full meaning of the conversa on.

Do not depend on just the hearing to pick up vital information. When you take your eyes off the speaker, you lose contact with the speaker. Read the chapter on lip reading to get more knowledge of the subject.

You must constantly remind others to look at you when they speak. They forget so fast but keep reminding them to face you when they speak.

3. The Mental Gate - We struggle so hard to grasp a conversa on. This is very exhausting and can wear a person down. Our attitude is crucial on how we interpret what we see and hear. We need stamina to endure listening to a lecture or a sermon.

We cannot take our focus off the speaker to make notes or read something. Breaking the line of communication sets us behind.

Casual discussions with one or two people is somewhat easy to follow. When there are three or more, the conversa on falls apart. It is important to get plenty of rest to get the most out of any social situation.

4. The Technical Gate - We will be discussing a wide variety of assistive listening devices to be used in the home, at school, in the theater, workplace, and the church. This is an exciting part of defensive hearing.

Regardless what type of hearing aids you have, you still need to consider alternative hearing assistive devices (ALDs).

5. The Heart Gate - Appreciate every person who is trying to help you hear better. Show love and others will want to love you.

This is a communication strategy that you must know, understand fully, and practice daily. I am not a genius or a scholar of any kind. The burden to communicate consumes me 24 hours a day. The more I learn, the more I want to help others with this amazing concept. This is by no means a scientific or scholarly treatise, but a very practical approach to better communication.

Stupidity pill

I dreamed that I invented a "Stupidity Pill." A better title is an anti-stupidity pill. It could get rid of all the stupid things you do and say. It will make you wise and intelligent in all the things you do and say. Life will be a lot better, and you will be very likable from now on.

The secret of the anti-stupidity pill is that you must confess openly that you have a stupidity problem. You must continue to let others know so they can help you do and say the right things. The more you follow this simple plan you, the better you will be liked wherever you go.

Those who reject the idea of such a pill will try to create substitute ways to make themselves wise and intelligent. Reading books on intelligence, taking up drinking, attending seminars, turning against God and start a sinful relationship, only leads to more stupidity.

To my surprise, no one would come publicly and get the remedy pill for stupidity. It would mean that they would have to admit the need such a pill. Some will say, "I am happy the way my life is. I can make it on my own without any help."

The only way the pill will work is to express your need for it daily. Sadly, the pill company went out of business for lack of sales. Is that stupid or what?

I have created a solution for people with hearing loss. The book on the Bill of Rights for Hard of Hearing contains a variety of ways to improve hearing and communication if you are willing to admit your need for it. Read on.

The Lord has led me to build a ministry for hard of hearing to advocate hearing accessibility in the church. We have installed FM systems for the hearing impaired. Many of the hard of hearing resist trying out a unit in church. It would make them feel stupid. What will people think of me if I plug into a hearing system to hear the Word of God?

The stigma of hearing loss is thought to be part of old age, mentally challenged, or low IQ. Rather than accept help, they will sit in church or class and never admit their own need to hear. They are not getting much out of service or the Bible study. They will pretend that everything is all right, but it is not.

They will seek alternative methods to improve their hearing. One method is to purchase a more expensive set of hearing aids that are invisible. That way no one will know that they have a hearing loss. Secondly, they will drop out of Bible class and church altogether.

Is that stupid or what? My family doctor said he could use the pill for himself and several members of his family.

Whenever I speak in a church about hearing loss, I ask how many of you have a hearing loss? Some people would raise their hands indicating they have a hearing loss. Then I would see several hands go up and pointing to someone nearby who did not raise his/her hand.

We must be willing to openly declare our hearing loss publicly. In the Bible, there is the story of a rich young man who came to Jesus and asked, "How can I have eternal life?" Jesus responded to keep the commandments. The rich young man explained that he kept all the commandments from his youth, then he asked, "What do I lack yet?"

Jesus declared, "Go and sell all that you have and give the money to the poor and come and follow me." He went away sad because he had great possessions.

A group of religious leaders brought a woman taken in adultery to Jesus. They asked for permission to stone her to death for her sin. Jesus knelt down and wrote in the sand. When he rose up, he said, "He who is without sin may cast the first stone." Jesus knelt down and wrote again. One by one all the religious leaders slipped away.

When Jesus looked up, everyone was gone except the woman.

Zaccheus was willing to publicly admit his need for the Lord's remedy for sin. His action of faith was to climb a tree, so Jesus would see him. Jesus declared, "Today has salvation come to your house."

The woman at the well-realized her sinful condition went into town and told everyone what Jesus had revealed about her life. Many people came out to receive the remedy for sin.

In our churches today, some people will not admit their need for salvation publicly and pay the price of spending eternity without Jesus Christ. Is that stupid or what?

Great Hope for Hearing Loss

When we focus on our handicap (disability),

we may drift away from God into what I call the "great hopelessness." We become a prisoner or victim of self-pity and seek isolation from society, family, friends, and church.

This book is not a medical thesis on depression. The solutions in this chapter may not sound scientific. When I get in a hole of despair, I try to find a way out. I look for alternative ways to overcome situations plaguing me. There is great hope for you.

While attending the morning worship service on Sunday, I sensed that I did not hear everything. I knew that I was missing 75% or more of the discussion in the Bible class. I tried to take in the message, but could not look up scripture, write outlines, hear, read lips and understand the message at the same time.

I realized that I had a serious hearing problem. I approached one of the pastors and told him my plight of not being able to hear. His only reply was, "There is nothing we can do to help you. Just do the best you can."

I turned around to walk out and began crying and muttered to myself, "There are 5000 members in this church and no help for people with hearing loss."

To deny a reasonable accommodation was an act of discrimination and a violation of the

American Disabilities Act. The ADA law was not known or made public to me until many years later. It felt like a hopeless situation, and I left the church, never to return.

My dear wife Cathy (who is hearing) showed me an article in a magazine about a television actor named Richard Thomas; who had a hearing loss and needed help. He played the part of John-Boy Walton in the Walton Family series on television.

Mr. Thomas discovered a national group called SHHH, or Self Help for Hard of Hearing and became active in a peer support and encouragement group.

After reading the article, we phoned the home office of SHHH in Bethesda, MD and were told that there was a local chapter meeting monthly at the Ronald McDonald House.

Members welcomed us warmly into the chapter. The meeting room was equipped with an FM hearing system and the telecoil loop system. A caption typist put all the words spoken on a big screen for everyone to see and hear everything.

Later, I served as president of the chapter, a rewarding experience. SHHH later became known as the Hearing Loss Association of America.

One of the meetings featured a psychologist who spoke on the "Steps of Grief" and how the grieving process affected friends with hearing loss. This lecture gave me much to ponder and high hopes for me to go on with my life. There is great hope for those who suffer hearing loss.

Discouragement and depression can sap a person's energy, leading to a state of hopelessness. It is easier to sleep a lot or stare at the TV and just do nothing. A pastor once said that depression periods recur annually or in a cycle. You can fight it by planning something that would keep you active and busy.

For me, it was the month of February when I struggled the most with depression. In some areas of the country when it snows or rains a lot of people may feel the blues.

While attending Bible School in Edmonton, Alberta, Canada, February was a tough time for depression or in this case "cabin fever." Days were short, and the nights were long. The snow just kept on piling up. We did not have money to attend sports events or other types of entertainment. Parlor games became boring.

A visiting speaker told us how he revived his spirit during the long winter months. He took off his shoes and went walking in the snow with bare feet. It was invigorating.

On Friday night, I asked the guys in the dorm if they would like to go for a walk. Several of us got dressed, left our shoes and socks behind and headed outdoors. The neighborhood was near a bus stop where people were waiting. We acted like nothing was different about us. Imagine Bible school students without shoes on their feet tramping in the snow.

That event perked up our spirits and gave us plenty to talk about. We returned to the dorm and soaked our feet in a hot tub of water.

February was a hard month in the ministry. A missionary friend asked me to help him at the Florida State Fair in Tampa. My wife and I started working at an evangelism booth for ten days each year. We stayed in people's homes, and all our needs were provided while there. We were given fresh oranges, grapefruits, kumquats, and strawberries to bring home.

There are things you can plan or do in your town without spending a lot of money. Visit people in a nursing home, shut-ins, or a senior center. Offer to help or serve. Look for ways to be a blessing to others, neighbors, or hospitals. Do anything that will take your mind off yourself.

Consider hobbies or crafts to create items for gifts or for sale. Do not wait for things to pop up for you to do. Go out and make things happen.

As a missionary, I worked bi-vocational to supplement our missionary support. Pushing myself to stay busy helped me. I painted, and pressure washed houses.

In my preteen years, Dad built a house for us. I was given the job of painting our two-story house one summer; a job that did not require hearing skills. The painting was a solo job that had many challenges and risks. Later I became an independent paint contractor.T he Lord enabled me to paint several houses for widows and people in need at no charge. It is better to give than to receive.

While painting houses, owners had materials and items in their yard and offered to pay me to haul them away. I brought home lumber, patio stones, yard furniture, windows and garden tools. With the excess material, I repaired our garage, built two patios, garden spaces, and improved our inside space.

Our house was built in 1930 and needed renovation. Our two sons did all the major carpenter work, and I did the finishing work and painting. My prize project was to remove the old open wood fireplace and build a river rock fireplace from the basement to the ceiling. The rock chimney outside was solid and was to connect to it.

It was a wonderful experience to work with my hands and be able to create a beautiful home for our family. Rather than mope and complain about things, I forced myself to stay busy with my hands to help others. To this day, I still have my down moments with my hearing loss, but I gained a great deal of satisfaction serving others.

You may not have a situation like mine, but you do struggle with hearing loss. You can find something to do besides watching TV. Opportunities are endless for you to come out from your discouragement and be a blessing. There is great hope for you.

A New Ministry

Not ready to go back to church and struggle through services, I felt led of the Lord to create a new ministry called "Flea Market Evangelism." To my knowledge, it had never been done before.

The calling from the Lord was keen to go, but I resisted for two days and nights. Finally, I surrendered to the will of God, and I went out to the garage and began building two gospel tract racks to display literature. The urge was to go to the local flea market. My thinking was, "What if this project failed? I would be the laughing stock of the town."

I decided to go where no one would know me to work in secret. With my pickup truck loaded, I headed for "Trade Day" near Collinsville. AL, seventy miles down the highway.

I intended to check into a motel for the night and set up the next morning. When I arrived, all 1000 vendor spaces were taken, and all motels were filled. The night manager informed me that, "if someone canceled, I could have that space. Come back around 4:30 or 5 o'clock a.m. and I will let you know."

I pulled into a parking area and moved the equipment over, so I could lie down. The floor was corrugated metal, and I was without a blanket or a pillow. "Lord," I prayed, "did I make a mistake coming here?" I did not get much sleep that night, but I did a whole lot of praying.

It was about 4 o'clock when I returned to the manager and asked if any space was available. He said, "no, but what do you need?" "All I need is some space to set up; I have a table, chairs, and displays". He pointed to a giant oak tree and said, "You can park there and set up."

As I began to set up, I felt guilty that I didn't tell the manager what I was going to do. Do I need special permission to pass out Gospel tracts and share the message of Jesus Christ?

People were coming in to set up their businesses. I found a café that was serving breakfast.

At 6 a.m. I was at my booth shaking in my boots and handing out Gospel tracts. During the morning, five different pastors came by with their wives. They were amazed to see a public display of the Gospel in a flea market.

It was a joy to share my story how I got here

and what the Lord led me to do. Each pastor was thrilled to see my boldness to witness for Jesus Christ. Each one of those pastors prayed over me and the display.

The reward came when two teenage girls came and asked me what I was doing. "Would you like to hear a wonderful story about how to get to heaven?" I asked. The thrill of it all was when they both bowed their head and prayed to receive the Lord Jesus Christ into their hearts and lives.

Rather than struggling through church services, I became the missionary pastor to the flea market. The following weekend I visited the Big D flea market in Dalton, GA. Arriving at 4:30 a.m. I set up under a large oak tree. This day was very fruitful beyond my expectation.

Twenty precious souls accepted Jesus Christ as Lord and Savior. Over time, several people joined me in this work. I never dreamed that God could use an uneducated Minnesota hillbilly preacher to lead others to Jesus. I am humbled.

If God can use me, He can use you to do great things for His glory. There is something that you can do.

It is common for people with hearing loss to work as independent contractors or to become self-employed. In those settings, we can avoid communication where the hearing is critical, such as handling phone calls.

In the flea market ministry, I could deal with people one on one or in small groups around a table. Using a visualized Gospel tract, it was easy to share the message of salvation. On several occasions, I met a person with a hearing loss. I loan them my pocket talker amplifier and an over the earpiece. The hard of hearing need to hear the Gospel message.

MAKE THE BIBLE YOUR SOURCE OF STRENGTH

My favorite book is the Holy Bible, the Word of God. My wife and I read through the entire Bible every year. We see how God worked in the lives of Bible characters who gained power from God through prayer.

In my personal life, I have claimed a verse or promise to bless me for the year. I find great strength and comfort from the eternal word of God. I love to hold the Word on my lap and read over some of the great passages that have blessed my soul. I favor a Bible with a leather cover and feel great joy and deep respect in holding a copy of the blessed book.

Today we can "google up" a copy of the Bible in any version or language. Clutching a smartphone and glancing at the tiny screen is not the same as holding a bound book.

The great hope and success comes from numerous attempts and failures. Success is never instant, but continuous progress a goal. Put your trust and hope in the Lord, and He will direct your ways to victory.

The Golden Rule

The Golden Rule for communicating with hard of hearing is as follows:

"Therefore, all things whatsoever you would that men should do to you, do even so to them: for this is the law and the prophets." (Matthew 7:12)

Go the extra mile. It will pay big dividends for you. What is your desire? What is your ideal or dream for effective communication?

Hearing loss is a communication problem. If we are as hard of hearing people are ever going to overcome the hurdles of hearing, we must learn to change the way we communicate. Change is threatening and difficult because we are in a rut in the way we do things. We develop a pattern of conversing that becomes easier for us.

It is our nature to want to get others to change; while we are not willing to change ourselves. We expect others to change their habit of speaking so we can understand them better. We have no clue how they need to change or what hearing people need to do to make themselves heard by us.

For years, I struggled with hearing loss and misunderstood a lot of what people were saying to me. I blamed them for my hearing problem. Hearing people need to speak up more and be more patient with me. Then it dawned on me one day that I need to change.

Change is always hard; in fact, it is nearly impossible to change an old habit. Mentally we think that change is too difficult to try. The truth is that change is really easy, once we understand why we need to change.

Once you establish the purpose or reason for the change, it seems easy.

Our goal is to get hearing people to change the way they communicate toward us. The best way to do that is to change the way we communicate to other hard of hearing people. Whoa, this is meddling. I have observed that hearing-impaired people do not follow any form of proper communication among themselves. The following are some simple steps that will help you communicate better.

1. Control your anger and frustration when others fail to get the message across to you. Don't blame others for your hearing problems and misunderstandings. Take a deep breath and ask yourself,

does that person know how to communicate with me? Have I taken the time to teach others the best method of speaking to me? What would it take to get others to speak to me, so I can understand it all?

Have faith that you can communicate properly with hard of hearing people. You can go from the depth of despair to the height of delight. You can rise from the pains of suffering to the gain of success. It's time to turn your scars to stars. Trust the Lord to give you wisdom and insight to overcome the struggles of hearing loss.

2. Stop acting like hearing people. Remember who you are, a hearing-impaired person among other hearing-impaired people. Accept the fact that we are hard of hearing and act accordingly.

Example: Stop calling to each other from different parts of the house. Do not continue a conversation walking away from hard of hearing person.

Do not interject your thoughts at random without getting attention first getting all the hard of hearing people to focus on you before you speak This concept may slow you down, but it is worth it. Do not assume that all hard of hearing people will know when you are speaking without letting them know.

This practice must last a lifetime. Begin doing it right the first time. The marriage would be much happier when the hearing spouse understands the best way to get the attention of the hearing-impaired mate.

3. Practice the Golden Rule of communication with hard of hearing people. Practice speaking the way you want hearing people to speak to you. Be the prime example on how to speak with and to you and other hard of hearing people. Set the example and stick with it

"Guided by justice and mercy, do unto all men as you would have them to do to you, were your circumstances and theirs reversed."

This command has usually been called the **Saviour's golden rule**, a name given to it on account of its great value. All that you expect or desire of others in similar circumstances, do to them. Act not from selfishness or injustice, but put yourself in the place of the other, and ask what you would expect of him then. It is easily applied, its justice is seen by all men, and all must acknowledge its force and value[14].

"This is the substance of all relative duty; all Scripture in a nutshell." Incomparable summary! How well called "the royal law!" (James 2:8; compare Romans 13:9). And the best commentary upon this fact is, that never till our Lord came down thus to teach did men effectually and widely exemplify it in their practice. The precise sense of the maxim is best referred to common sense.

The meaning of this rule lies in three things.

(1.) We must do that to our neighbor (as well as hard of hearing) which we acknowledge to be fit and reasonable: the appeal is made to our judgment, and the discovery of our judgment is referred to that which is our own will and expectation when it is our case.

(2.) We must put other people upon the level with ourselves, (such as hard of hearing) and reckon we are as much obliged to them, as they to us. We are as much bound to the duty of justice as they, and they as much entitled to the benefit of it as we.

(3.) We must, in our dealings with men, suppose ourselves in the same particular case and circumstances with those we have to do with and deal accordingly. If I were making such a one's bargain, laboring under such a one's infirmity and affliction, (with a hearing loss) how should I desire and expect to be treated?

Christ came to teach us, not only what we are to know and believe, but what we are to do; not only toward God but men; not only toward those of our party and persuasion but toward men in general, all with whom we have to do. We must do that to our neighbor, which we acknowledge to be fit and reasonable.

Whatsoever do ye even so to them. This

does not imply that we are always to do to others as they wish, but what we would like to have done to ourselves if we were placed in their condition and they in ours.

Luke 6:31 "And as ye would that men should do to you, do ye also to them likewise."

For even sinners, said he, do the same: men who do not regard God at all. Therefore, he may do this, who has not taken one step in Christianity.

Hearing impairment needs not to drive a wedge between couples or family members or friends. Striving together to find a proper solution can make any relationship stronger and happier.

The hearing-impaired person as well everyone associated with that person needs to be involved in a total program of rehabilitation.
- Understanding the range of hearing aids
- Using assistive listening devices
- Practice speechreading
- Art of listening
- Being assertive
- Training others how to communicate with the hearing impaired
- People who wear hearing aids still has trouble understanding words
- Treat all hearing people as if they were hearing of hearing. Act as if you are helping

them in a kind and compassionate way. It could become contagious and be a real blessing to everyone.
- You are teaching hearing people how they are to respond to you.
- Express gratitude for the slightest improvement and help from others.
- Thank you for getting my attention first and facing me when you speak, I appreciate that.
- Thank others for not shouting, or over enunciating their words. Speak in a normal tone of voice.
- Appreciate others when they repeat things back to you.

I am sure that all the hard of hearing people in this meeting appreciate this helpful communication. If I were the only hard of hearing person in the world, I would keep quiet, but in every meeting or gathering of people, several will have a hearing problem. Thanks for thinking about us.

It is so kind of you to be conscious of the hard of hearing people in your group, class, and church. I realize that it is hard for you to change a pattern of communication, but is wonderful when you take the time to include me and us in the group, study or conversation.

David M. Harrison

Mission Fields in America

How many people do we need to constitute a mission field? What is a mission field? Where do we find them? Are there any more mission fields in America, or are they found only on the far side of the globe?

We all have our definition of a mission field. Where there is a need, that is a mission field.

The church seems to think they have exhausted the possibilities of serving on a mission field in America. My goal in this paper is to expose the need of serving in a local mission field in our area.

Illiteracy-42 million -Forty-two million adults in the United States cannot read, write, or do basic math above a third-grade level. What is their greatest need? To learn to read. Illiteracy is an enormous unreached mission field that is invisible. People who cannot read do not attend Bible studies and church to avoid the embarrassment of being called on to read a passage. There has to be a way to get these people into church that does not require reading. They can be saved without reading the Roman Road. For centuries people were taught the Word of God and did not have a written copy of the Bible.

Many of our good Bible classes today are

taught on a seminary level by great scholars and Bible students. Each member is expected to do collateral reading and prepare to participate in the discussion. People who cannot read can still love God and have a testimony to share with others.[15]

Hunger-49 million - One in six people in America face hunger. The USDA defines "food insecurity" as the lack of access, at times, to enough food for all household members. In 2011, households with children reported a significantly higher food insecurity rate than households without children: 20.6% vs. 12.2%.

Forty-nine 49 million Americans struggle to put food on the table. In the US, hunger is not caused by a lack of food, but rather the continued prevalence of poverty.

We cannot see hunger, but we know it is there. Hunger is a daily problem and feeding a few children, or people occasionally does not take away hunger the rest of the time.

This is an invisible mission field before us that needs much help every day.[16]

Poverty-43 million - The official poverty rate is 12.7 percent, based on the U.S. Census Bureau's 2016 estimates. That year, an estimated 43.1 million Americans lived in poverty according to the official measure. According to supplemental poverty measure, the poverty rate was 14.0 percent.

The U.S. Census Bureau defines "deep poverty" as living in a household with a total cash income below 50 percent of its poverty threshold. According to the Census Bureau, in 2016 18.5 million people lived in deep poverty. Those in deep poverty represented 5.8 percent of the total population and 45.6 percent of those in poverty.

While poverty thresholds vary by the size and household composition, for a single individual under 65 years old, deep poverty would be an income below

$6,243 in 2016. For a family of four with two children, it would be $12,169.50.

Poverty is a mission field.

Hispanic-52 million - The demographics of Hispanic and Latino Americans depict a population that is the second-largest ethnic group in the United States, 52 million people or 16.7% of the national population. Forty-seven million Hispanic Americans are citizens.

They are also the nation's second-fastest-growing racial or ethnic group, with a 2.0% growth rate between 2015 and 2016 compared with a 3.0% rate for Asians. The slowing of Hispanic population growth is occurring as immigration to the U.S. from

Mexico levels off and the fertility rate among Hispanic women declines.[17]

African Americans-42 million

There were 37,144,530 non-Hispanic blacks, which comprised 12.1% of the population. This number increased to 42 million according to the 2010 United States Census, when including Multiracial African-Americans, making up 14% of the total U.S. population.[18]

Homeless Americans-553,742 - There are an estimated 553,742 people in the United States experiencing homelessness on a given night, according to the most recent national point in-time estimate (January 2017). This represents a rate of approximately 17 people experiencing homelessness per every 10,000 people in the general population.[19] Housing for the homeless is a mission field.

Deaf Americans-500,000 - American Sign Language (ASL) is a complete, complex language that employs signs made by moving the hands combined with facial expressions and postures of the body. It is the primary language of many North Americans who are Deaf and is one of several communication options used by people who are deaf or hard-of-hearing. Apr 25, 2017[20]

Although the precise number of ASL users is

difficult to determine, ASL is the predominant language – in other words, the language used most frequently for face-to-face communication, learned either as a first or second language – of an estimated 100,000 to 500,000 Americans (Padden, 1987), including Deaf native signers, hearing children of Deaf parents, and adult Deaf signers who have learned ASL from other Deaf individuals.[21]

Approximately 2 million people in the United States cannot understand normal speech, and of this number, just under 500,000 comprise the deaf community (deaf people who use sign language).

Census statistics on languages spoken in the home, published in "Characteristics of Population by Ethnic Origin." The number of deaf persons using sign language is approximately 500,000.

Hard of Hearing-48 million - Statistics: About 20 percent of Americans, 48 million, report some degree of hearing loss. At age 65, one out of three people has a hearing loss. About 2-3 of every 1,000 children in the United States are born with a detectable hearing loss in one or both ears. [22]

*Approximately **15%** of American adults (37.5 million) aged 18 and over report some trouble hearing.*

Men are almost twice as likely as women to

have hearing loss among adults aged 20-69.

Non-Hispanic white adults are more likely than adults in other racial/ethnic groups to have hearing loss; non-Hispanic black adults have the lowest prevalence of hearing loss among adults aged 20-69.

One in eight people in the United States (13 percent, or 30 million) aged 12 years or older have hearing loss in both ears, based on standard hearing examinations[23].

Consider the 10-40 Window of missions: the largest unreached mission field without the Lord Jesus Christ.[24]

*The **10/40 Window** is a term coined by Christian missionary strategist Luis Bush in 1990 to refer to those regions of the eastern hemisphere.*

The European and African part of the western hemisphere, located between 10 and 40 degrees north of the equator'. This general area in 1990 was purported to have the highest level of socioeconomic challenges and least access to the Christian message and Christian resources on the planet.

Africa has 1,243,265,000 people in 50 countries with 3694 people groups where only 15% are Christians.

Asia has 4,584,390,000 people in 58 countries with 7,387 people groups where only

2.8% are Christians.

Less than 3% of all the missionaries in the world serve in the 10/40 window with less than .01% of all mission money spent to reach this area of the world.[25]

Ministering to Shutouts

We have overlooked people with special needs in the church. After visiting many churches, I met people, heard their stories, and understood the need that has not been addressed. The church can minister to friends with hearing loss.

Many men and women achieved great works for God and humanity, but sacrificed financially, socially, health-wise, and neglected their own families. I challenge you, pastor and church leaders, meet the needs of your church family and reach out to others in need. In 1995 I dropped out of church, feeling **shutout** from our church people. I assessed what I understood in Sunday school and church. In church, I understood no words sung by choirs or in a special number, and no prayers since most folks bowed their heads and I could not lip read. If the pastor turned his back to speak to the choir or if he paced back and forth, the message was lost to me. I depend on seeing the face of the speaker and trying to read lips.

Friends invited us to join a mission board that works with Deaf people. We learned American Sign Language (ASL) to communicate. Working in the Deaf community was a difficult step in culture and linguistics since I am neither "full Deaf" nor fully hearing and my wife is hearing. We did not feel accepted by the Deaf or by the hearing. The deaf could not comprehend the idea of being hard of hearing. You are either deaf or hearing, but not in between. We served six years. No accommodation was ever made for the hearing impaired only.

Where can I go from here? Where can I find a community of hard of hearing Christians that understand my needs and be a blessing to them?

I sought a hearing-friendly church. Every church we visited had a silent group of friends who suffered hearing loss and communication struggles; from 10 to 17 % of each church. When I shared my dream with them, many wept and begged for help.

In 2004 the Canadian Association for Deafness (CAD) did a survey of feeling **shut out** from public and private life due to hearing loss. 82% reported they felt **shut out** from family events and conversation. 88% said going to theaters and sports events were difficult.

80% dropped out of church or stated they could not hear well enough to attend. 94% stated struggling to hear is stressful and exhausting in public and at home.

Many have not shared with people that they have a hearing loss and need help in communicating. Why so silent about a hearing disability? Several reasons exist:

First: hearing loss may be invisible, and others may not know your need.

Second: a stigma is attached to telling others about hearing loss, being labeled as retarded or senile. I felt ashamed to admit I could not understand others.

Third: we don't know why we can't understand what others are saying. Hearing aids should help yet sounds are garbled. We make blunders and say things not pertinent to the present conversation. Communication breakdowns persist.

Fourth: we cannot tell hearing friends how to communicate with us, so we suffer in silence and miss much.

Fifth: Some hard of hearing continue in church because family members are there.

In our visits to churches, we found a few with a ministry to one or two Deaf persons in the main service. A trained interpreter would use ASL if a Deaf person showed up.

We found several churches with assistive listening devices (ALDs) for hard of hearing. Church members were not aware of this service project.

Bill of Rights for the Hard of Hearing

Some church leaders knew they had units but could not find them; some units were broken, had dead batteries, or were not turned on.

We found one church in town with real-time captioning on a computer screen for the main morning service.

Of the many churches we visited, more than 40 pastors had hearing loss, including a Jewish rabbi and son. These pastors seemed to assume that they were the only hard of hearing members of their churches.

I spoke to Sunday School classes and groups of seniors and shared from the pulpit. After the service, hard of hearing friends gathered around me and shared their needs. Pastors felt shocked to see a group gather but were not prepared to pursue a ministry of helps.

Did they **shut out** the hard of hearing by attitude or lack of concern?

My wife and I attended a mission conference where a missionary from Vietnam spoke, demonstrating the six tones of one vowel. I asked him later how deaf or hard of hearing folks deal with a tonal language. His response broke my heart. "In our country, if a person is not whole or has any physical defects or deformity, he or she is an outcast and becomes a vagabond."

They were **shut out** from society.

Another missionary shared that he wanted to start a Deaf ministry in a third world country. He visited a small village and asked where deaf people could be found. He was led out behind the village and saw several wooden makeshift cages. Inside each one sat an unkempt person who was deaf. The Nationals feared the deaf since they could not communicate with them.

They were **shut out** from family and society.

Does this situation exist in the United States of America? Up until the 1960's, Deaf and hard of hearing were placed in prisons or mental institutions. When I entered first grade, I was placed in a special education class for Deaf and hard of hearing for eight years. I was later told I was classified as mentally retarded, incapable of learning, and mentally incompetent.

I was **shut out** from an education.

Does discrimination exist today in our society? We may be ignored or shunned or called names when we make a mistake in communication. We become the butt of jokes or ridiculed or accused of "selective hearing."

We were invited to visit and speak at a country church near Mars Hill, North Carolina. A young pastor assured me that every member of the church was hearing. While I visited with the pastor, two elderly ladies shared their stories with my wife Cathy, a nurse.

My wife relayed the stories to me, and I asked the ladies if I could share with the group. The ladies had been in the church for decades and loved their pastor, the church, and its family. The dear ladies came to church faithfully

"hungry for a blessing but went home empty." The young pastor looked dismayed but did not know what to say.

They were **shut out** from the church.

It is now time to start a ministry in the church to reach the hard of hearing in the community.

A Peer Support Ministry

People with hearing disability need to have a support group that understands their needs.

When I attended the Self-Help for Hard of Hearing (SHHH) meetings, I made an important discovery. The leaders invited speakers to give lectures that may or may not relate to hearing loss. In early days, we would head to the dining hall for refreshments. We would push tables together for close fellowship.

What happened around the table made an impact upon me. We shared our struggles and problems that we face daily. It was a sharing time of how we dealt and overcame a hearing situation. It was a fun and open conversation that made the meeting significant. Many times, I would say to myself, "I learned something that helped me."

When I was teaching Lip Reading, I felt the need to have a fellowship and sharing time after the class. We began a monthly meeting on Friday evening for anyone to come and bring something to eat. It was called the Hear Now Café, a peer support group. We learned from each other by sharing stories about our lives with hearing loss.

There are support groups for addictions, cancer survivors, and widows. The Hear Now Café can be a group of any size that meets for sharing and prayer.

Hearing loss can hit at the very core of our being because it limits our ability to communicate with those around us. You enter into a lonely communication vacuum from the hearing world when you cannot hear. People don't understand how to deal with one who has a hearing loss.

You long to share how you feel about being left out of a conversation. You desire to be able to talk about your disability, but the subject becomes annoying to the hearing people. Where can you find comfort and understanding?

You don't have to suffer in silence anymore. Start your support group with one or two people.

Share your struggles without complaining about what others won't do for you. Discuss ways to encourage one another on how to deal with your hearing dilemma.

The term that I have used is "Peer Group Therapy" for the Hear Now Café and is a concept for treating depression. It works to solve problems and change unhelpful thinking and attitudes. We glean experiential knowledge on specialized information that people obtained from living through a unique hearing situation. This knowledge is pragmatic and when shared, contributes to solving an individual problem and improves their quality of life.

The effectiveness of peer support is believed to derive from a variety of psychosocial processes described best by Mark Salzer in 2002:

- The helper-therapy principle proposes that there are four significant benefits to those who provide peer support:
- Emotional Support (esteem, attachment, and reassurance)
- Instrumental Support (material goods and services)
- Companionship
- Information Support (advice, guidance, and feedback).
- The Hear Now Café concept is a relaxed

atmosphere of fellowship with friends who experience hearing loss. We offer healing and hope to continue in life. The conclusion of each session ends with prayer.

Stories that Heal

When my wife and I served as missionaries in Alberta, Canada, I desired to hear stories told by the Cree Indians.

I collected stories of wisdom, battles, animals, victories; lessons in life from the people, and their history and legends.

Telling a story provided an opportunity to gain understanding from one's experience. I saw these stories as messages of salvation that could help children accept Christ as Savior.

My collection of stories was presented at summer camps, Vacation Bible Schools, and rallies across the country. Applying a gospel message to my stories created a great platform for giving an invitation to children to receive Christ.

Today, stories can be shared to bring healing to those who grieve. Poetry, drama, films, art, music, and singing can set the tone for the grieving process. Folklore is filled with thoughts that help ease grief by therapeutic storytelling.

Stories of disabilities in life can help the storyteller and the listener. A friend with hearing loss needs to share his story and feel accepted by the group before he can move forward in life.

A dying Aids patient spoke to his counselor, saying, "If you don't mind, I'd like to tell you my life story. I am dying, and there isn't anyone to tell it to. I can't die until I have told you the whole thing. Will you listen?"

A professor at the University of Alberta in Calgary stated that an illness or a handicap is a call for a story. Stories may be perceived as helpful to those in distress. Healing can affect both the storyteller and the listener.

Tell us your story.

Your hearing loss is unique. No one has experienced hearing loss exactly like you have. No one knows the depth of pain in your life. Your story can bring comfort and strength to others.

This book is a collection of ideas on how to survive the hearing loss dilemma; your survival kit to guide you in this chaotic world of hearing. We hard of hearing people (HOH) are hurting and seeking solutions to improve our communication skills.

We learn by hearing our own story, watching the reactions of others, and experiencing our story being shared. Some friends don't want to hear our story and wonder if we truly suffer when our handicap seems invisible. Quest stories meet suffering head-on. They accept the hearing loss and use it to seek survival. We can learn from that.

"Our stories will develop into the story of God. Redemption must become part of our hearing loss disability. God has a purpose for you and wants to bless you and others."

In the Gospels, we read stories of people who were healed. Each, in turn, shared the story of his good news with others. Even though you were not healed, you can discover the power of God in your life.

The joy of the LORD becomes a powerful message for others to receive the Lord Jesus Christ as personal Savior.

In "A New Paradigm of Evangelism,"
Leighton Ford states that "the story produced a vision, which then transforms character, resulting in evangelism. This provides a clear, workable, biblical pattern for effective, natural witnessing."

Making the church hearing accessible for friends with hearing loss becomes a new paradigm for evangelism. When you realize there are 50 plus million Americans with mild to moderate hearing loss, that is an untapped mission field at our door.

The concept of evangelism today has lost its steam. We have run out of ideas to get Christians to bring visitors to church to hear the Gospel.

We are on the verge of a whole new approach to evangelism. Hearing loss is everywhere among people we know and see regularly. Most of them are church dropouts.

Creating a hearing-friendly atmosphere in

the church gives us an opportunity to invite hard of hearing friends without seeming pushy. Understanding what hearing accessibility is and having literature on hand is an easy way to reach others. We are targeting a special needs group of people who want to hear the word of God clearly in the church.

The Hear Now ministry is an exciting and easy method for church members to practice without embarrassment. This plan could spread like wildfire, creating interest and a desire to test the church sound system.

This book will help you survive the hearing loss dilemma and give you a story to tell. Tell about God's redemption in your life.

Others will gladly hear you and may accept an invitation to receive Christ personally.

My story: on December 20th in 1999, I flew to St. Paul, Minnesota to preach the funeral message for my twin brother. It was a sad time in my life, and I needed comfort to handle the loss of my brother. Was the LORD dealing with me about something? It was Christmas week and bitterly cold: four below zero with a 45 below zero windchill.

On the day of the funeral, I arose at 5 AM and decided to go for a walk in the fresh snow.

I sensed the presence of God. Suddenly I felt or heard the beautiful tones of a harp. The music seemed to come from above me, yet I could hear the sounds within my heart.

As I focused on the music inside me, the story of David's Amazing Harp was revealed to me. Peace flooded my soul, and the tranquil surroundings heightened the joy of it all.

My heart was lifted up to God in thanksgiving for the comfort and gift of sweet peace. I wished that everyone could experience such precious inner peace.

I realized then that even in the midst of death there was perfect peace in my heart. I believe this is the true meaning of Christmas, and peace is the gift the world seeks.

The story of David's Amazing Harp was printed and given to scores of friends who were grieving. My story tells of the harp music that soothes, comforts, and brings healing to the soul.

This story tells how David the shepherd boy and later king of Israel wrote Psalm 23.

Open Hear Policy

I created the Open Hear Policy of the Bill of Rights for The Hard of Hearing and patterned it after the Sunshine Law in government, which says: *"The sunshine legislation makes provision for the laws, regulations, contracts and other deals done by the state and its employees, elected and non-elected, to be documented and made completely open to the public and the press."*

The Open Hear Policy is in compliance with the American Disabilities Act of 1990 to provide complete hearing accessibility for the hard of hearing in all meetings in public and church. The need is to feel included in all activities.

In a nutshell, the **Open Hear Policy** is stated as:

To make sure that every hearing-impaired person can see, hear, and understand everything that goes on in every meeting.

To give every hard of hearing person the opportunity to be heard and understood. The FM hearing devices and loop system must be available whenever possible. Captioning will be offered only in the main assembly room.

The guidelines are straightforward and easy to follow. When hard of hearing people are in any meeting, they must stop acting like hearing people by speaking up whenever they feel like it. The policy is designed to include everyone, hearing or hard of hearing. They are as follows:

- No one talks unless acknowledged by the leader
- Do not talk until you have the microphone
- Give full attention to the one speaking
- Be respectful of the speaker

- Listen to their stories and discussions
- Do not dominate the conversation

To make the guideline functional, every person must be able to see who is speaking. In small groups, sitting around tables or in a circle is helpful. Even with hearing aids and the microphone hooked up to the FM system, it is still difficult to hear some speakers. It is important that we see the speakers face for lip reading.

The purpose of the Open Hear Policy is fivefold:

To demonstrate the highest level of respect and accessibility for hard of hearing friends present. It will help everyone feel close to each other.

To create a flow of communication. Each person can add valuable information for all to benefit. We do not want to exclude anyone by our criticism or remarks. To be sympathetic and kind to others who share their heartaches and trials to the group. Everyone is having a tough time.

Listen to their stories. To build a relationship and relieve tension when we have a loving spirit. Many of us have few real friends to accept us with hearing loss.

To build our friendship by ending all meetings with prayer for one another.

When people with hearing loss are present, we must practice the open hear policy. That means we become an advocate and assistant to make sure every person with hearing loss is included and hears everything being discussed.

It is important to acknowledge when a hearing-impaired person is present. Do not assume that he hears everything fine. Do not treat the person as mentally challenged. When a message is not heard correctly, it takes time to figure out what was said. There may be a confused look on his face.

He may respond to a question not fully understood and give an answer that has nothing to do with the subject.

Never make a joke about the answer or call the person a name. Understand the person has lost his hearing not his I.Q.

With hearing loss, it is difficult to follow a discussion or conversation of more than two people. Help him get on track by interpreting or repeating the subject matter. As a person with a hearing loss, learn to assert yourself. Explain that you are hard of hearing and that you are not sure what the discussion is about.

The Open Hear Policy is all about making sure the conversation is accessible to all our friends with hearing loss. Let us practice this in class. We want to feel included in every activity.

We have not begun to uncover, discover and develop all there is to accommodate the hearing impaired.

The Magic Button

The MAGIC "hearing" BUTTON was created for friends who need help to hear. The button has no power in itself to restore hearing. The formula behind the button can work wonders for all who apply it to their daily lives.

When you need to hear better, it may not be more gadgets, surgery, medicine, or technology, but rather a unique technique. The magic button can increase your ability to communicate.

The most expensive hearing aid in the world may fail to bring back your hearing. Extra hearing equipment may disappoint you.

Take time to read this chapter several times so you can grasp the concept and put it into practice.

- Develop a bold attitude to become an assertive advocate for your hearing loss.
- Draw attention to the magic button to take the focus off yourself.
- Tap on the magic hearing button to explain your need to hear and understand.
- Tell the story of the button, so people will listen and assist you.
- Create hearing awareness

As a hard of hearing person, your challenge is to create hearing awareness by advocating your hearing loss. Share the need for hearing accessibility for yourself and others.

Be proactive when people communicate with you. The magic button works with or without hearing aids. Hearing aids are not a cure for hearing loss, and most have a limited range. Do not depend only on your hearing aids to give you maximum hearing.

Four things may happen when you wear the Magic Button.

1. Well-meaning people may raise their voices and yell at you. Inform them that they do not need to yell because you have volume control on your hearing aid.

2. Friends will ask why you don't learn sign language which would help you. The question is; who will speak to me in sign language?

3. People may ask why you don't get a cochlear implant. Most insurance does not cover that operation which is very expensive. It takes a long time to understand sound and speech after that surgery.

4. Some will offer you condolences — "Oh, you poor thing! I am so sorry for you."

Make the Button a Teaching Tool. Know

what and how you want people to communicate with you. Explain that the magic button prompts them to look directly at you and then speak.

Face Me I Lip Read.

When a person loses hearing, his eyes serve as ears. Ask a person to come closer and speak to your eyes. Your communication level will rise. Have fun wearing the Magic Button Wear the button all the time and let it advocate for you. The button can be read from 5 or 6 feet away. In a doctor's office or noisy restaurant, tap your button to get attention. People will look and get the point.

Never Hide your Hearing Loss. Hiding your hearing loss compounds your communication problem. Your family and friends already know you have lost hearing.

Move past the stigma and fear of what people may think. Hearing loss is not a sin, sign of senility, old age, or retardation. It is present in every age group, nationality, and culture. It occurs in the rich and poor, wise and unwise, and every class of society.

Take these steps to better communication:
- Receive the button and pin it above your heart.
- Study the manual to gain knowledge.
- Develop the story you want to share.

- Practice until your story becomes second nature.
- Test on family or friends until you feel comfortable.
- Perform—tell your story wherever you go Start gradually and work on your project.

Persistence makes the impossible possible. Order form is in back of book for buttons. Visuals to help others understand:

- I carry a hole-punched laminated card in my billfold and can wear it on a cord around my neck if I am a patient in the hospital. I ask each person entering my room to read the card stating my need.
- Mini-stickers: I created ½ inch adhesive stickers which say Face Me—I Lip Read. I stick one of these on the bridge (nose piece) of my glasses to invite folks to step closer to me to read it.

Message to Hard of Hearing Friend

For greater accessibility, you are responsible to:
- Understand your hearing loss: what, how, when?

- Know what will help you hear better.
- Teach others how to communicate with you.
- Never fake or bluff that you hear okay.
- Do not ignore the fact that you did not get the message.
- Train yourself to know when understanding goes astray.
- Stop conversation or teacher and make needed adjustment.
- Ask the speaker to face the light.
- Move away from the noise to a quiet place.

The Story of the Magic Hearing Button

The Magic Hearing Button of communication is not just a neat little item to wear, but a powerful story to share.

You can confidently face the hearing world with a whole new attitude. Learn the story of the Magic Hearing Button and how it can help you.

Here is the story: Relay your personal hearing challenge to others. The magic hearing button shows three things:

I. The button displays the international symbol of hearing accessibility in the background.

    a. Information - The color blue indicates information listed in the drivers' manual. Other items are the emergency evacuation routes and wheelchair accessibility symbol.

    b. **Announcement** - I need assistance to hear; I am hard of hearing.

    c. **A legal warning** -The American Disabilities Act was updated in 2010 with stricter guidelines. Public venues must provide reasonable accommodation for those who are disabled. When a request for accessibility is rejected, it can now be subject to a lawsuit.

    d. **A bold confession** of your hearing loss. Most people listen and want to help you.

II. The button has two statements in the foreground.

    b. **FACE ME** is a command or request:

This is an instruction for the speaker to speak to your eyes. *"If I don't see your face, I cannot hear you or understand your words."* My eyes serve as my third ear.

    c. **I LIP READ** an explanation: As a hard of hearing person, you focus intently on any speaker who approaches you. When your hearing goes down, you automatically read people's faces. The statement gets the person in the right position for better communication; within three to five feet of you, with good lighting.

III. **Develop your Presentation** about your disability

Bill of Rights for the Hard of Hearing

a. Personalize your story. What type of hearing loss do you have? How long have you been hard of hearing? What caused the loss? Do you have tinnitus or ringing of the ears?

b. Which ear is better?

c. Do you wear a hearing aid?

d. How do you want others to speak to you? Normal or Loud?

This is the international symbol of access for hearing loss. Along with the wheelchair symbols, they are the only two "official" adopted international handicap symbols. The hearing loss symbol deals with communication.

The logo shows a side profile of a human ear with a thick line that runs diagonally through the ear. The pictogram indicates that an assistive listening system is available for use by hard of hearing. The symbol represents the ramp to better communication called hearing accessibility. This symbol has been drafted into law with the American Disabilities Act (ADA) in 1990.

The Magic Hearing Button has this symbol in the background to show that you need special attention. The story you share must be your personal need for people to respect your request to see, hear and understand everything spoken. The ADA covers all forms of disabilities, including deaf and hard of hearing. Hearing loss is the largest handicap group in the world. Our plea is to be included in all activities and conversations.[26]

This button may boost your communication skills. You will have hearing problems the rest of your life. No matter how much you spend on technology, there is no perfect solution.

My advice is to stop pretending you can hear perfectly and understand everything. Hearing loss is often gradual. You may think other people are mumbling when they speak to you.

The blame game has to stop when you realize you have trouble hearing others. It may take up seven years to do something about your situation. When you go to the doctor, you may be told you have permanent damage. Hearing loss is invisible to others. If your hearing aids are not obvious, you may need to identify yourself as a person with hearing loss.

People need to look directly at you, so you can see their face. Teach this principle everywhere you go.

If communication is important to you, you must tell others how to help you understand them. Be bold, not timid, and prompt others with, "Could you speak up? I cannot hear you," or "Could you repeat that, please?" Instruct people how they can help you understand.

You have to look at the face of a clock to tell time. I need to see your face to understand what you are saying.

I created the magic hearing button and wear it in public: it is a big help to me. The button is 2 ½ inches across and says, "Face Me, I Lip Read."

I Cannot Change the Way I Talk

IT IS A LONELY WORLD for friends with hearing loss and almost impossible to follow a conversation. To ask people to repeat themselves becomes a burden. The hearing people get upset when they have to slow down and repeat to accommodate you. We are forced into isolation and loneliness because no one understands our need to hear.

Does being alone away from people make you lonely? I do not think so. Being surrounded by family, friends and loved ones who grow weary assisting a person with a hearing loss; that is lonely indeed.

Separation from family and friends can be the deepest kind of loneliness.

While serving as a missionary on an Indian reservation, I was called to bring a mother to the hospital to discuss her one-year-old baby who was dying. The baby had not developed physically and refused to eat. The Doctor explained to me that the baby was dying for lack of love.

"He has no will to live because no one touched or kissed him. He will not be alive by morning", the doctor predicted.

A dear grandmother who was in the hospital asked if she could hold the baby and try to feed him. She held the child close to her breast, rocked him back and forth and hummed songs. Soon the infant responded to the love given and began drinking and eating.

Dying for lack of love

Who are the lonely ones today? The elderly, widows, poor, outcasts, bullied, single parents, and hard of hearing. They feel rejected and feel that no one cares.

Let me paraphrase two passages from the New Testament:

"Let love be your greatest virtue toward others. Aim to practice spiritual graces such as longsuffering, gentleness, goodness, faith, meekness, patience, and kindness without limits."

Practice these on everyone to edify, uplift, and encourage the lonely. This act will help those who are having a difficult time communicating.

Why do children tease those with a handicap?

Sadly, teasing happens also among adults.

They imitate the disability in a rude way to show what they think of you. It may be a superior attitude to say, "I am better than you." People can be unkind toward an individual with a disability.

My experience as a hard of hearing meant that when I wear my body type hearing aid. It is a small, powerful unit the size of a deck of cards on a lanyard around my neck.

People say to me, "Why don't you get a real hearing aid?" My response is, "You mean like the ones that cost thousands of dollars and hide inside the ear, so no one will know I have a hearing loss?" Those tiny units do not have the power to accommodate my profound hearing loss.

Lynn Johnston, creator of the beloved cartoon "For Better or Worse," featured a story about a girl with a cleft palate. I quote the text here from the Tues, June 20, 2007, issue:

*"You...tease...me...about...the way... I... talk...I was born... with... a... cleft...palate... they... couldn't... fix... it... un l...I...was...four! I... had... to... speak...all...over...again...and...that...i s...why...I...talk...like...this. I...can't... change... the...way...I... talk... but... you... can...**change... the... way... you... LISTEN!**"*

You can change the way you listen was the best lesson about communicating with her.

With the hard of hearing the lesson can be changed to, "You tease me for the way I hear and misunderstand you. I was born hard of hearing and cannot change the way I hear you, but you can change the way you SPEAK TO ME." My hearing loss will never go away. There are many ways and strategies you can practice when speaking to me.

My experience of being teased about hearing loss was in the form of bullying. As an adult, grown men seemed to think that my hearing aid was a toy or a joke and yelled in the microphone to see if I could hear. These painful moments were hard for me to handle. Asking them to stop seems to excite them to do it again. The worst part is that this was taking place in church by men in ministry (missionaries). They had no respect for disabled hearing people. There were eight men who thought it cool to pick on me. We could not resolve the issue and left the church. We did counsel with several and wrote a letter of concern to the pastor. The attitude did not change.

My PKT Amplifier Story

My first hearing aid was awarded to me in a drawing at the Minnesota State Fair in 1950.

It was a body unit worn on my chest with a halter strap under my shirt. It was a "Sonotone 910" chrome plated with a gold belt clip. The unit had an inbuilt microphone and a wire to an ear mold piece for hearing. It was equipped with vacuum tubes.

Later I got a behind the ear (BTE) hearing aid, which broke down several times, and had to be sent away for repairs.

The microphone picked up more noise behind me than in front. Several things that annoyed me were outbursts of laughter, wind blowing in the microphone, coughing, and clapping. These noises were like shotgun blasts.

Controlling the volume was the most difficult part when sudden noises occurred. At that moment I decided that the next hearing unit was going to be another type of body aid, so I could control it instantly.

Around 2000, I discovered the Pocket Talker (PKT) personal amplifier by Williams Sounds, Co. It was the same size as the Sonotone 910 unit but more powerful. (The size of a deck of cards.) My hearing journey advanced tremendously. There were many advantages and possibilities that made my hearing more accessible. The price was very reasonable that fit my budget.

Here is a no-frill hearing instrument that met my needs personally. It was a thrill to wear this unit every day. I wanted to explore many possibilities to see what this amazing technology could do for me. There were few instructions what could be done, but I love to experiment. Here are some of the advantages of the PKT personal amplifier:

- Durability: This unit has a five-year warranty that will be fixed or replaced. The triple "A" batteries lasted more than 200 hours. It felt like five weeks to me.
- Instant control: Without fumbling for the control button. The fastest turn off was to pull the detachable microphone out.
- Power: This unit had the power for the most profound hearing loss. It never let me down. The lowest volume on the unit was powerful enough for me a number of years. As my hearing decreases, the volume can be turned up to meet my needs.
- Visibility: I do not try to hide my hearing unit. It is worn on the outside of my chest with a lanyard. The microphone needs to be out front for better communication.
- Practical: Can be operated with one hand and very hard to lose.

- Multiple options: Many types of earpieces, microphones, and loop for "telecoil" users.
- The PKT personal amplifier met the requirement of American Disability Act, ADA).

The use of the microphone can enhance your hearing tremendously if you are willing to use it strategically. By that I mean get as close to the speaker with the microphone as possible. This is difficult with hearing aids which are stationary on the side of the head.

Remember this, the microphone in any hearing aid is best served when used within six to twelve inches of the speaker. This is not possible when we are three to five feet away.

An example: the telephone or cell phone has to be close to the speaker's mouth for the listener to hear you.

In an auditorium where the speaker on the platform who uses a microphone, he or she must keep it close to his/her mouth. If he/she moves more than a foot away from the podium, the people will complain.

Your hearing aid works on the same principle. If the speaker is more than three feet away, you may be out of earshot, and communication becomes difficult.

This causes a lot of frustration to hearing aid

users because it is assumed that the price paid should do the job clearly, up to ten or twenty feet away. Bilateral hearing aids should even be better. NOT SO!

I discovered this problem when I fastened my PKT personal amplifier on my belt. I could not hear my own voice at that distance. Hearing improved when I placed my unit on a lanyard around my neck.

The significant feature of the PKT personal amplifier is the removable microphone. There is a wide selection of microphones you can choose. With an extension cord, I can now understand people in noisy crowds. What I love is that each earpiece has a forty-inch cord that I can hold out to speakers and read their lips at the same time.

This is a demonstration of love of hearing accessibility that has put me in touch with my friends. Around a conference table, I place a special Omni directional conference microphone [MIC049] in the middle of the table that makes it easier to follow a conversation of several people up to eight to twelve feet away.

I was working at an indoor flea market handing out Gospel tracts and talking to people about the Lord. A couple came by; I asked them if they would like to see a presentation on how to go to heaven. The wife agreed and came in and sat down. The husband moved away from the booth and stood there. I asked, "Why didn't he come in?" She responded, "Oh, he's hard of hearing and can't hear."

"I have a surprise for you," I said. Taking my earpiece out and adding an extension cord to my PKT personal amplifier, I invited the man to come and listen. He was amazed when he heard the gospel message clearly in a noisy place.

This type of **love demonstration** can be done for home visitation by church leaders. Medical personnel can use this unit in hospitals, nursing homes, and doctor's visits. When hearing situations prove challenging, the PKT personal amplifier delivers. There are three different PKT models:

- PKT D1 Ultra Personal Amplifier
- PKT Pro Personal amplifier (not as versatile)
- PKT 2.0 Personal amplifier

A hearing aid is a customized medical device that amplifies all sounds and is stationary on your ear.

The Personal amplifier is used to amplify specific sounds or voices. You control what you want to hear by reducing distracting background noise. This can be done by using different microphones and extension cords.

David M. Harrison

Benefit of the Pkt Personal Amplifier

My personal amplifier has become the lifeblood of my communication. It has become a great boost when hearing aids are not strong enough.

Most small hearing aids are designed to serve mild to moderate hearing loss. The PKT personal amplifier is powerful enough to serve the severe to profound hearing loss.

It is an easy-to-use portable unit that can improve your ability to communicate in situations where hearing is difficult.

Extension Cord

With an extension cord, the PKT Personal Amplifier becomes a great television listening device. The best place that I use this item is in motels when traveling. There is rarely a comfortable place to watch the TV. Now I can watch without disturbing the neighbors in the next room, and my wife can sleep peacefully in the same room.

At home this method is a marriage saver, we can enjoy a program with the volume low enough for her. Otherwise, she could not be in the same part of the house. I know a couple who got divorced over this issue. This is a very sensitive and simple **demonstration of love** for both the hard of hearing and the hearing.

This PKT is very versatile that makes hearing accessible a joy. It benefits the hearing people who normally talk very loud to me.

Riding in the Car

Communication in the car can be a big challenge. With the extension cord, my wife can have the microphone clipped to her lapel or seat belt. This prevents me from having to look at her to read her lips while driving at high speed in heavy traffic on a curve.

Assist for Hearing Aids

I have the cochlear implant in my right ear and a $10,000 "Phonak" hearing aid on my left side. Believe it or not, I still struggle to hear clearly what others are saying.

It's no wonder I depend on my PKT unit to fill in where I need it most. Using a small book carrying case, I can take it everywhere I go with extra batteries. There are so many places I encounter that the implant and the hearing aid doesn't help much. You cannot depend only on the equipment you have. This may be hard to believe, as for me it is the truth. This statement may hurt a lot of people who insist that their product is the final answer for better hearing.

I care more about your hearing. It matters to me. You deserve to know how to cope when hearing become difficult. Too many of my friends have dumped their present hearing aids thinking that the more expensive ones work better. They are very disappointed over this move.

While attending the American Association of Audiology, one audiologist rebuked me and told me to get a real hearing aid. After attending many other conventions, no one ever approached me or talked to about getting a cochlear implant.

The PKT personal amplifier was never meant to be your main hearing device. I wore this unit for ten years and was satisfied with it.

While attending the International Federation for Hard of Hearing in Washington D.C., the cochlear representatives challenged me to get rid of the amplifier and get the implant. They registered my name to go to Vanderbilt University for testing in Nashville, Tennessee.

After hours of testing and interview the doctors scheduled me for surgery December 20, 2016 and was activated on January 5, 2017. The road to recovery was difficult because I suffered vertigo for a month. Any noise coming into the right side set off the vertigo. I began walking with a three-prong cane and staggered like a drunk person. I felt like a hundred-year-old man.

The company advised me to wear the implant every day until you hear perfectly. Two audiologists told me that it would take a year or more to get adjusted. I am in too many situations and group meetings to be patient.

The Dream to Hear

The dream to hear in church did not come to a head until 2006. I was born with a profound loss of hearing. The public-school system placed me in special education classes in St. Paul, Minnesota for mentally challenged.

In those days there was little distinction between hard of hearing and mentally challenged. Learning was not a priority, because it was thought we were incapable of learning.

When I got to the ninth grade, I dropped out of school. I was passing all the grades with A's, but not learning. This has impacted my ability to spell, do grammar, and math. These are handicaps that have followed me all my life. Looking for a job was difficult.

A new junior high school was built in South St. Paul where I lived, so I went to the principal and insisted he let me, mainstream regular classes. I graduated from high school in 1955. During these years I got a job washing dishes in a small dinner and later became a short order cook.

After high school, social workers made it possible for me to attend several training institutes for a job. All were too difficult for me to continue due to spelling, grammar, and math. I got a job as an office boy at the Internal Revenue Service and later became the printer for tax forms. I discovered that I work better with my hands than with my head.

I became a Christian on New Year's Eve 1958 and heard the call for my life to "full-time Christian service." I desired to serve the Lord in some capacity.

This was the dream and hope all my life. In September, I enrolled at Bethel College where I met my future wife, Cathy Hart Brown. After two years of college, I enrolled at a new Bible Institute in Edmonton, Alberta, Canada.

Cathy and I married in 1963 after she finished her RN training and moved to Edmonton to finish my senior year. We began our mission work on the Cree Indian Reservation near Red Deer, Alberta, Canada.

After years of missionary service on several fields, we settled in Chattanooga, Tennessee. I traveled as a children's evangelist conducting crusades.

My final dream mission did not begin until 2006. God had put a dream in my heart, but I did not relate it to hard of hearing people. In my moment of discouragement, I needed direction to finish out my days on earth.

God has prepared me for a dream mission

since birth. I have always felt that I was destined for some great cause to change the world. I have tried many times to make my dream come true with different business adventures and ministries. They all failed in a sense because it was not God's final mission for me. Several of these ministries were fruitful.

You cannot go looking for that specific mission that God has for you. You have everything needed to do God's greatest dream for your life. Take your eyes off yourself and look for a great need in others that you know only you can fulfill. When it becomes a passion that you know pleases God, you know you are on the right track.

Using the Bible as my guide, I selected Mathew Chapter six to help me develop the ministry. Three simple principles were easy to follow. Number one was giving to others in secret. Number two was to pray in secret. Third, was to fast in secret.

What you do in secret, God will reward you openly. This has been proven many times and still works today. To find my dream ministry did not come easy for me. I was desperate for God to show me His plan for my life.

I was motivated to seek the Lord with all my heart. It was time to get a hold of God for answers. It was a simple plan that did not require any money or going to a specific place. I decided to take two weeks to pray and fast until God moved me. Fasting is one way to show God that you are serious about seeking His will.

Several books came across my path as I began my quest for that big dream.

The most important book in my life is the Holy Bible. Cathy and I have read through the whole Bible every year. Every day after breakfast we would take time to read several chapters. How precious is this marvelous book, with its eternal treasures?

The first book that made an impact on my life was, "The Dream Giver" by Bruce Wilkinson © 2003, Multnomah Books. This book became the blueprint for helping me pursue my dream. In the introduction, he states, "I will be your coach to reach your dream."

The second book that opened the world of prayer for me was, "The Prayer of Jabez" by Bruce Wilkinson, © 2000.

Third, the Complete Works on Prayer by E.M. Bounds © 2004 have been an inspiration to me.

The fourth book, "Fasting" by Jentezen Franklin © 2004 that put fasting in a proper biblical order. His ideal passion was to fast for twenty-one days at the beginning of every year.

The fifth book was the "Secrets of The Vine" by Bruce Wilkinson © 2001. A book on holiness. The sixth book that has challenged my life was, "Acres of Diamonds" by Russell H. Conwell, 1960, Temple University.

My dream mission is God's perfect will for my life. Anything I do to advance the Kingdom of God produces great honor and glory to God Himself. This, in turn, brings great rewards of unlimited abundance and blessing for my family and me.

While pursuing the dream for my life, I came across a website from the *American Academy for Hearing Loss Support Specialists. (http://www.hearingloss.org/content/hlsst).*

The academy offered online training to become an advocate for hearing accessibility and help hard of hearing deal with the struggles of hearing loss. My wife and I enrolled in the academic studies of reading hundreds of papers online and ten books. We finished the course in July 2006. The more I read, the more I became excited about what God was leading me into. I saw a great need to be dealt with by helping people with hearing loss. The excitement increased when I got to the last book I needed to read.

The course taught me about my struggles with hearing loss. I related to ways to overcome many of the hearing loss situations and how it could

David M. Harrison

help others. The last book was on *"Speech Reading" by Harriet Kaplan, Scott J.*

Bally and Carol Garretson ©1985, Gallaudet University. This book covered lessons on lip reading. I am convinced that many others would benefit from this one book alone.

When the year 2007 rolled around, I had in place a program to start the Lip Reading Academy in Chattanooga. We began our first classes in February once a week for eight weeks. Twenty students came to this class.

Acres of Diamonds

We do not have to travel the globe to remote countries to discover new mission fields. There are pockets of people that are not hearing the Word of God within and outside the local church. One of those untapped mission fields is the hard of hearing people that has grown to more than 50 million.

From 1900 to 1925, Russell Conwell told this story called "Acres of Diamonds" over 5000 times.

His story told of a wealthy farmer who sold everything he had to pursue diamonds. After years of searching the farmer spent all he had and died a beggar. The man who bought his farm found a large stone in the nearby creek. A neighbor recognized the stone as a diamond. The owner denied that it was a diamond, but just a pretty stone. Together they ran out to the creek to discover more diamonds.

This place, known as the Kingdom of Golconda in India was the most lucrative diamond mine in history, excelling the Kimberly mine of South Africa. Had the farmer stayed home he would have discovered "Acres of Diamonds" in his own backyard.

There are mission fields or acres of diamonds of people in need all around the church that have not yet been discovered. One of those undiscovered fields is the **hard of hearing people**. People with hearing loss are the largest disability group in the country.

Ruth Stafford Peale suggested to her husband that he **find a need and fill it** as the simplest way to start a great ministry. Find a hurt and heal it or find a problem and solve it.

Great mission works started by meeting specific needs of a few people. Schools, churches, hospitals, rescue missions, and orphanages all began with the desire or passion to help others in need.

Hearing loss has become a serious disability that needs to be addressed. Every church in America has a pocket of people that suffers from hearing loss and needs assistance to hear the Word of God clearly. These people are the real acres of diamonds whose needs can be met so they can be a great asset to the church.

Taking the time to minister to the needs of the hard of hearing within the church can lead to reaching the tens of thousands outside the church. It is estimated that 85% of the 50 million hard of hearing Americans do not attend church because the church is not **hearing accessible**. Behold the fields are white unto harvest in your backyard.

Before any work can begin to meet the need of a pocket of people, we must change our attitude about ministering to them. Hard of hearing people are not retarded or senile. There are loved ones, church members, relatives, neighbors, and friends that you know with a hearing problem. They want to hear clearly the Word of God in every service and department of the church.

The rate of dropouts among hard of hearing members is high. This can be reversed by creating a hearing-friendly atmosphere to draw them back into the fold. **Hearing accessibility** can meet a great need for all hearing members who have been hurt and feel rejected or neglected.

Becoming **hearing accessibl**e can heal a lot of hurt and resolve a big problem to bless many. We must revitalize the church within its membership by ministering to the hard of hearing first before we can reach out to the thousands outside the church.

> **Until the Trumpet Sounds,
> LET MY PEOPLE HEAR!**

David M. Harrison

My Dying Wish for you

I don't know how much longer I have to live, but I have a dying wish for you before you die.

My greatest wish for you is that you will accept Jesus Christ into your heart and life so that you can go to heaven. Making that decision is the greatest thing you can do for yourself and me personally.

This eternal decision will change your life forever. I urge you to decide today before it is too late. We never think of dying but think we will live forever. "I have plenty of time to make that decision," you might say. Death may come to you sooner than you expect.

God loves you just as you are and cares about your soul. I cry out to you in desperation. Do it now! It is a critical matter because time may be running out for you. Do not let your past sins keep you from making that decision this moment.

When you confess your sins to God, He will forgive them all and remember them no more. "God is faithful and just to forgive us of all our unrighteousness." "Seek ye the Lord while He may be found, call upon Him while He is near."

If you die without making that decision, you cannot change your mind later.

All decisions are final.

There will come a day when you cry out to

the Lord to save you. But He will not hear your cry. It is too late. Without Jesus Christ in your heart and life, you will be eternally separated from the love of God.

Your decision today is a matter of eternal life in heaven or eternal death in the lake of fire.

To accept Jesus Christ into your heart today means eternal life, joy, and peace forever.

I urge you to pray and ask the Lord to save you today.

There may come a time, "when your fear comes as a storm and desolation, and your calamity comes on as a whirlwind when distress and anguish come to you. Then you will call upon God, but He will not answer, you will seek

God early and diligently, but you will not find Him." Proverbs 1:27-18

Jesus said, "Today is the day of salvation, now is the accepted time." "Seek you the LORD while He may be found, call upon Him while He near: let the wicked forsake his way, and let him return to the LORD, He will have mercy upon you, and to our God, for He will abundantly pardon." (*Isaiah 55:6-7*) Make my dying wish for you a jubilant victory of personal salvation. Satan cannot destroy your soul once you invite Jesus Christ into your heart. This is not time for procrastination, but for an urgent choice.

I am gravely serious about your salvation. I will not give up on you until the day I die. Don't put off this decision, because delay could be a disaster for you.

The moment you make that decision for Christ, your name will be written in the Lamb's Book of Life. This is the only record that God has to prove you made that decision.

Romans 9:2-3 "I have great heaviness and continual sorrow in my heart. For

I could wish that myself were accursed (separated) from Christ for (you) my brethren."

You may already know God's plan of salvation for you. You hunger for something to take away that emptiness in your life, to give you that peace you are searching for, and give you great joy and happiness in your soul.

Your decision is a pressing and critical matter because time is running out. I am forcefully pleading and making a strong recommendation for you to accept Jesus Christ today.

In other words, "asking" is not what saves. A person must "believe," or trust that Jesus paid for his/her sins on the cross, was buried and rose again from the dead on the third day.

Let me help you make that decision. Pray something like this:

"Lord Jesus, I believe you are the Son of

God, born of a virgin, grew up without sin, and was crucified on the cross in my place. You suffered, bled, and died for my sins. You were dead for three days and arose alive from the grave, victorious over death.

I now believe and accept you as my Lord and Savior forever. Thank you for giving me eternal life. Amen"

More information on Captioning

This chapter deals with other uses where captioning may be found around the world.

Technical helps are available for hearing impaired friends. Churches have technical equipment installed and in use and can add a few extras to minister to hard of hearing effectively.

Closed Captioning

When you purchase a DVD, you see the symbol CC meaning closed caption.

Words are synchronized with speaking and background sounds mentioned, which eases frustration for hard of hearing.

The term "closed" in closed captioning means that not all viewers see the words, only those who decode or activate them.

Closed captioning is used in noisy public environments such as bars or restaurants, where patrons cannot hear over background noise, or where multiple televisions display different programs.

Speed Typing

In a meeting with hard of hearing, communication is difficult without captioning.

A visible form of the spoken word is needed. Find a member or volunteer to type the speech on the computer and use a projector to flash words on the wall or a screen. The type can be enlarged for better readability. Our goal is to help everyone attending to see, hear, and understand everything.

Open Captioning Movies

Open-captioned movies ensure that all patrons can enjoy films, even Deaf, and hearing-impaired friends. Producers include all dialogue plus sound effects and song lyrics.

Real-Time Captioning

Real-time captions are created at the program origination. They are encased in white letters with a black background. They scroll up to three lines at a time and come after double chevrons (< >). Real-time captioning is used for lectures, such as a training seminar, corporate meeting, sports event, or "live" events that do not allow time to prepare the captions.

Subtitles

Subtitles are textual versions of dialogue in films and television programs, displayed at the bottom of the screen. They can be a written translation of a foreign language or local language, with or without added information such as background sounds or song lyrics.

At film festivals, subtitles may be shown on a separate display below the screen.

Stage Texting

Stage texting is an exciting feature for those who love the theater. This new concept in America is widely used in Europe.

Text light boards are used in advertising, at bus stops, to direct traffic, and on marquees. The lettering is orange or yellow and visible at a distance.

In a theater, the text board may be mounted for all to see but not to interfere with actors. The entire script is programmed into a computer by a captionist and operated on cue during the play. The words are on the board in little bubble lights, a beautiful sight to my eyes.

All operas are captioned on a screen above the stage. Operas in foreign languages are displayed in English.

In New York City, more than a dozen productions are captioned on the light board.

This service may be offered at only one showing in the series, so call ahead to find the right date for you.

In England, choices are unlimited. Several

theaters list the captioning group: Chickenshed, RSC, Theatre Royal. Most are captioned in-house.

The Hampstead Theatre in London offers a post-show discussion of the show using speech to text transcription.

All public building in the United Kingdom, including theaters, museums, and movie houses, must install the telecoils loop system for those who wear hearing aids with a "T" switch. This service is required by the federal law similar to our American Disabilities Act.

The Tate Modern Museum in London offers a person palm pilot for tours for users of British Sign Language.

Subtitled Cinema

For those who enjoy movies, "The Guardian's Saturday Guide" of the United Kingdom lists each month over 1000 subtitled screenings in 250 cinemas or theaters. Listings cover England, Scotland, Wales, and Ireland. Listing is also in the newspapers and on the internet: www.yourlocalcinema.com.

Australia has the second largest selection of movies and plays listed at www.mediaaccess.org.au.

David M. Harrison

Cinema Audio Description

This is a fantastic service for people with visual impairment. The film soundtrack comes through speakers, and a recorded narrator explains the play through personal headphones, like listening to a sports game on the radio. You feel you are in the middle of the action.

Most cinema releases are now available with audio description files. More than 300 United Kingdom cinemas have facilities to "read" these files.

Get the Script

What if you cannot attend a play on the caption-available date? What if you visit a school or church drama and know you will not understand the words? All plays have copyrighted scripts. Go to the public library and get a script or arrive early and ask for a copy of the script. Carry a small penlight to the event. Enjoy the play!

C-Print Captioning

C-Print is a speech-to-text (captioning) technology and service developed at the National Technical Institute for the Deaf, a college of Rochester Institute of

Technology. The system successfully is being used to provide communication access to

individuals who are deaf or hard of hearing in many programs around the country. In addition to educational environments, C-Print also can be used in business and community settings, and with individuals with other disabilities, such as those with a visual impairment or a learning disability.
https://www.rit.edu/ntid/cprint/

The basis of C-Print is printed text of spoken English displayed in real time, which is a proven and appropriate means of acquiring information for some individuals who are deaf or hard of hearing. A trained operator, called a C-Print captionist, produces a text display of the spoken information in a classroom or other settings. At the same time, one or more students read the display to access the information. A C-Print captionist includes as much information as possible, generally providing a meaning-for-meaning translation of the spoken English content. After class, the text can be provided in paper or electronic format for the student to use as notes. (ibid)

The Technology

C-Print Pro software is specifically designed for providing C-Print speech-to-text services. It allows a captionist to input text using a keyboard abbreviation system. The abbreviation system is based on phonetics, or how words sound. Although spelling-based abbreviations might seem easier to learn, in practice, abbreviations based on how words sound are more instinctive because unlike traditional keyboard typing, a C-Print captionist processes information auditorily. Typing using abbreviations based on how words sound is an extension of the auditory process. Also, problematic spelling is not an issue. The software also can accept input from automatic speech recognition applications.[27]

Acknowledgment

To **Cathy Hart Harrison**, a registered nurse, my dear sweet wife of 55 years, who feels the challenge of living with my hearing loss. You are my dearest friend and partner in ministry. Thanks for proofreading the manuscript. You are the crown jewel of my life.

To **Angie Fuoco** for her kind assistance, counsel, and advice. She is our guest editor and advocate for hearing accessibility, and cares for hard of hearing people, and a dear friend of ours.

To **pastor Ken Clark,** who has become a wonderful prayer partner. We meet every week for prayer, those have been great moments in my life.

To Oakwood Baptist Church for accepting us into the fellowship. The members have been so kind and loving.

To the men who operate the Hearing Center. **Tom Albro** is one of the nicest member to work with, so helpful and good-natured. His happiness drives some people crazy. **Adair Park** is the technical person and keeps everything running smoothly.

Special thanks to **Ron True**, men's Bible teacher. I was a stranger, and you took me in. You made it possible for me to be in the Bible study and helped me to hear in the classroom. You are dear friend, prayer partner and advocate for hearing accessibility. You are a great inspiration to me. Thank you.

To all those who attended the lip-reading classes. Thanks for your input into the discussions.

To all hard of hearing friends everywhere. Come and join us in our "I Want to Hear" Campaign.

Books published by David M. Harrison

The Hour of Decision, Tract © 2018 By Cathy Hart Harrison
Lord, You Know I Can't Hear! © 2015
The Law of Total Accessible Communication © 2009
Witnessing for Jesus ©2001
David's Amazing Harp © 2000
God's Master Plan to Reach Every Creature ©1998
Mount Calvary in Psalm Twenty-Three © 1998
Platform Vacation Bible School Manual © 1994
How to Get Rid of Mildew on Siding © 1992 (a trade manual)
Dynamic Mission Deputation © 1986
Can You Find Your Way to Heaven? Tract © 1978
How to Conduct a Platform Bible School © 1975

Works Cited

1. National Association of the Deaf
2. h ps://en.wikipedia.org/wiki/Manually_coded_language
3. http://www.wisegeek.com/what-are-the-characteristics-ofa-healthy-respiratory-sy...
4. (Wikipedia)
5. Beginner's guide to lipreading
6. "Get American Sign Language(asl.)"
7. https://www.nad.org/resources/technology/captioning-for-access/when-is-captionin...
8. Retrieved from ttp://support.typewell.com/customer/en/portal/articles/1909341transcribing-vs-captioning
9. http://www.docsoft.com/Resources/Studies/Whitepapers/whitepaper-ASR.pdf (accessed April 18, 2016).
10. IR Remote CART Services - Edmonton Court Reporter, http://edmontoncourtreporter.com/educationalcart.htm (accessed April 18, 2016).
   http://tfwm.com/opening-up-services-with-closed-captioning/ Retrieved from Technology for Worship Magazine
11. https://www.wikihow.com/Text
12. http://www.nsc.org/safety_road/Distracted_Driving/Pages/DDAM.aspx
13. This report from the Governors Highway Safety

Association offers more information
14. http://classic.studylight.org/com/bnn/view.cgi?book=mt&chapter=007
15. h ps://www.proliteracy.org
16. DoSomething.org
17. http://pewrsr.ch/2wBy0qS
18. https://en.wikipedia.org/wiki/Race_and_ethnicity_in_the_United_States
19. https://endhomelessness.org/homelessness-in-america
20. https://www.nidcd.nih.gov/health/american-sign-language
21. (Wilcox & Peyton, 1999, p. 1)
22. www.hearingloss.org/content/basic-facts-about-hearing-loss
23. https://joshuaproject.net/
24. http://www.ad2000.org/
25. https://joshuaproject.net/
26. This is copyrighted material and is given permission by the author to reproduce it.
27. Rochester Institute of Technology National Technical Institute for the Deaf 52 Lomb Memorial Drive Rochester, New York 14623-5604 585-475-7557 (Voice/TTY)585-475-5949 (Fax) cprint@rit.edu http://cprint.rit.edu

Author's Profile

David M. Harrison was born profoundly hard of hearing and is dependent on lip reading. After semi-retiring, he felt that life was over, and he dropped out of church because it was not hearing accessible.

Pondering his future, in 2006, he began 14 days of prayer and fasting. God opened the way for him for training to become a Hearing Loss Support Specialist and founded the Lip Reading Academy. He wrote his first book: Lord You Know I Can't Hear.

While teaching at the Academy for ten years, many of the students complained that the church was not accessible for hard of hearing. It was then he knew that the book**: "Bill of Rights for the Hard of Hearing"** had to be written.

The Bill of Rights for the Hard of Hearing is the guideline that recognizes the unique communication needs for the hearing impaired in the church. No hard of hearing person should be deprived from hearing the Word of God in the house of worship. It is a disgrace and a shameful thing to be disabled with a hearing loss and feel ignored.

Hearing loss is an International Human Rights and Health Issue. This book announces the

Christians God in the church. We must challenge the church to make some changes to accommodate hard of hearing.

He is calling all hard of hearing friends to unite together with him to ban all forms of discrimination in public venues and Houses of worship. David lives with his wife of fifty-five years in Chattanooga, TN. They have three children and eleven grandchildren. He loves to cook and is a folk artist using antiques and junk items.

His passion is studying the Bible and spending much time in secret for prayer.